Peculiar Baking

MAGIC IS THE SIMPLEST
OF INGREDIENTS.

A Practical Guide
to Strange Confections

Peculiar Baking

Nikk Alcaraz

Creator of Practical Peculiarities

PAGE STREET
PUBLISHING CO.

PAGE STREET
PUBLISHING CO.

First published in 2024 by
Page Street Publishing Co.
27 Congress Street, Suite 1511
Salem, MA 01970
www.pagestreetpublishing.com

Distributed by Macmillan, sales in Canada by The Canadian Manda Group.

28 27 26 25 24   1 2 3 4 5

ISBN-13: 979-8-89003-020-7

Library of Congress Control Number: 2023949683

Edited by Elliot Wren Phillips
Cover and book design by Emma Hardy for Page Street Publishing Co.
Photography by Weston St. James

Printed and bound in China

DEDICATION

For my grandmothers, George and Yvonne, from whom I've inherited
the gifts of curiosity, cleverness and creativity.

TABLE OF CONTENTS

A WORLD OF PECULIARITY

Peculiarities exist in every corner of our lives. From the artful pattern on a spider's web to celestial happenings in the sky, the world is brimming with peculiar wonders. With willing eyes and a bit of imagination, it can be experienced everywhere, anytime and every day of the year.

My fascination with peculiarities and baking began as a child. I was raised by my grandmother, who loved Halloween, witches and all peculiar things. It was with her that I gained many skillsets, like crafting, hosting, storytelling and, most importantly, baking. Baking with my grandmother was always a euphoric experience. The way she would make the most amazing cookies just by eyeballing the ingredients was pure magic to me. No measuring cups, no fancy equipment. Just her hands and the complete intention that whatever she was making was going to turn out perfectly. It always did. . . . except for this one time when things didn't go as planned. She made me swear not to tell anyone, but now that she has been gone for many years, I believe it's okay if I tell you this little peculiar secret.

Years ago, on an evening before Christmas, Grandma and I were making her famous cookies, called biscochitos. This anise-flavored shortbread is a staple in Santa Fe, New Mexico, and my grandma was known for her version. Everybody expected a platter, so we had to make many batches to give as gifts. We were baking all through the night, all while snacking on these delicious cookies. We finished around 9:00 p.m., and she was on her way to bed. I stayed up and was tasked with making mini banana bread loaves, which required me to sift the flour. As I was sifting, I noticed big chunks of flour that didn't make it through the sieve. Upon closer inspection and to my surprise, there were a handful of dead beetle larvae caught in the sieve. I immediately ran to show my grandma. We looked at each other in shock because we had been snacking on those cookies all night. She had me throw all the batches of cookies away. All the hours of hard work we had put in was gone in seconds. The big bag of flour that we had bought was speckled with these creepy crawlies. She had me run to the store before it closed to buy a fresh bag. We then stayed up until 3:00 a.m. to bake all new batches for the next day. We were so tired that all we could do was laugh about what had just happened. It was then that she made me swear not to tell a soul. I suppose this gives her ghost permission to haunt me now.

This peculiar moment is one I will never forget, and I write it here so I never do. This moment triggered my imagination and inspired me in many ways. The fact that in the dead of winter before Christmas I was able to experience something that felt reminiscent of a Halloween prank was so cool! After that, I'd often ask myself how I could add the same element of surprise and uncertainty into my own food. How to make something taste delicious, look questionable and tempt the tastebuds all at the same time. Through the years, I've tested various strange recipes and techniques in the name of peculiarity. I invite you to get inspired by the beauty that lurks within the shadows, eat a few chocolate beetles and maybe even have a full-on conversation with a devil's food cake. These pages are packed with strange tips and tricks to create peculiar masterpieces for all year long. It's all in good fun, as long as you remember to sift the flour.

TIPS FOR SUCCESSFUL CONJURING

Baking is much like casting a spell. They both require specific ingredients, steps and a great deal of focus with the intent of bringing about a desired outcome. In this book, you will learn to create an array of peculiar treats. Some recipes are quite easy, and some may look intimidating at first glance. Magic takes practice, so follow the steps as written and you will surely succeed. Here are some helpful tips for successfully conjuring the desserts in this book.

Read through the recipe before beginning. This will help you determine if you have all the right ingredients, tools and time to complete the recipe.

Gather all your ingredients beforehand. Most recipes require you to combine them in a timely manner. Having everything pre-measured and ready to go helps reduce any mishaps.

Measure your ingredients properly. Each recipe has the ingredients written by cups and by weight.

> **Measuring cups:** A liquid measuring cup is for all liquids. Scoop measuring cups are for dry goods. They are not exactly interchangeable.

> **Scale:** Measuring by weight is the most accurate and consistent. I recommend it, especially for bread making. Measuring by weight also requires fewer dishes.

> **Flour:** The number one issue that can arise in baking is adding the incorrect amount of flour. This usually happens when a baker measures by cups instead of using a scale. When measuring by cups, excess flour gets packed in, which can lead to dry baked goods. To measure flour properly with cups, measure the amount you need and sift it onto a piece of parchment paper. Then lightly spoon the flour into the measuring cup and level off the flour with a butter knife.

Measure out a level cup of unsifted flour.	*Sift the flour through a sieve onto parchment paper.*	*Lightly pile the flour back into the cup.*	*Level off the cup with a butter knife. You will see that there are a couple of tablespoons leftover after sifting.*

Temperature matters. Following the suggested temperature of ingredients is crucial to the outcome of a dessert. Mixing cold eggs with room temperature butter won't incorporate well, and not using a thermometer when making caramel can turn into a sticky situation.

Use quality ingredients. It's better to opt for the best quality ingredient of the main flavor in a recipe. For example, the best quality chocolate chips can really take a mediocre-tasting cookie to a cookie that's to die for!

Have patience. Food art takes much longer than whipping up a normal batch of something. Make sure you have enough time to complete the project.

Be persistent. If you don't get it the first time, try again. Even if it doesn't turn out as fanciful as you'd hoped, it will all taste good in the end.

A TRICK FOR FILLING A PIPING BAG

Fold the piping bag over a tall cup.

Scoop the contents and close the bag.
The cup acts as a third arm and helps to avoid a mess.

Cursed Cakes

"Once bitten, forever bewitched."

DEVIL'S FOOD CAKE

A WORD OF WARNING TO THE BRAVEST SOUL: SUMMONING THIS CAKE MAY TAKE ITS TOLL. TO THOSE WHO ATTEMPT IT, BEST OF LUCK, FOR IF CONJURED INCORRECTLY, IT WILL RUN AMOK. A WORD OF ADVICE I KNOW TO BE TRUE, BITE THE CAKE FIRST BEFORE IT BITES YOU!

Yield: 1 (6-inch [15-cm]) three-layer cake

....

Moist Chocolate Cake

2 cups (250 g) all-purpose flour

¾ cup (55 g) Dutch-processed cocoa powder

2 tsp (9 g) baking soda

1 tsp baking powder

¾ tsp kosher salt

1¾ cups (350 g) granulated sugar

2 large eggs

1½ tsp (7 g) vanilla extract

¾ cup (173 g) full-fat sour cream

¼ cup (55 g) milk

1 cup (224 g) vegetable oil

1 cup (212 g) hot black coffee, freshly brewed

Italian Meringue Buttercream

8 large egg whites

½ tsp cream of tartar

2¼ cups (450 g) granulated sugar

⅔ cup (158 g) water

½ tsp kosher salt

3½ cups (795 g/7 sticks) unsalted butter, softened

2 tsp (8 g) vanilla extract

2 tsp (12 g) white gel food dye (optional)

Preheat the oven to 300°F (150°C). Spray three 6-inch (15-cm) round cake pans with nonstick baking spray.

MOIST CHOCOLATE CAKE: In a bowl, whisk together the flour, cocoa powder, baking soda, baking powder and salt. Add in the sugar, eggs, vanilla, sour cream, milk and vegetable oil. Mix until combined. Slowly add in the hot coffee and mix; the batter will be watery. Pour the batter evenly between the three cake pans. Tap them on the counter to release any air bubbles.

Bake the cakes for 60 to 70 minutes, until a toothpick comes out clean. Let the cakes cool for 15 minutes, then flip them onto a parchment-lined cooking rack to cool completely.

ITALIAN MERINGUE BUTTERCREAM: Place the egg whites into the bowl of a stand mixer with the whisk attachment and sift in the cream of tartar. Set it aside.

In a saucepan with a lid, mix the sugar and water until combined. Place the pan over medium heat, add the lid and bring to a simmer. Let it simmer for 5 minutes—this helps prevent the sugar from crystalizing. Remove the lid and continue to simmer the sugar without stirring.

When the sugar reaches 235°F (112°C), start beating the egg whites on high speed and add the salt. The egg whites should begin to look foamy like shampoo and have soft peaks. Lower the mixer to medium speed. When the sugar reaches 240°F (115°C), slowly stream the hot sugar syrup into the foamy egg whites. Try to pour the syrup in between the bowl and the whisk to avoid splattering. Turn the mixer to high speed for 10 minutes, until the mixture looks like marshmallow crème and it comes to stiff peaks. Scoop the meringue onto a parchment-lined baking tray and place it in the freezer for 10 minutes to allow it to cool faster.

(continued)

DEVIL'S FOOD CAKE *continued*

Chocolate Ganache Filling

1 (11.5-oz [326-g]) bag semi-sweet chocolate chips

¾ cup (178 g) heavy whipping cream

Rice Cereal Treats

1½ tsp (8 g) melted butter

44 mini marshmallows

¾ cup (25 g) rice cereal

Modeling Chocolate

1 (12-oz [350-g]) bag white melting chocolate candy wafers

¼ cup (84 g) light corn syrup

Gel food dye (black, purple, red, pink, yellow, brown)

6 maraschino cherries with stems, for topping

Special Tools

3 (6-inch [15-cm]) cake pans

Cake leveler

8-inch (20-cm) cake board

Piping bags

Paintbrushes

Star piping tips (Wilton #16, #18, #32)

Ruffle piping tip (Wilton #70)

Cake smoother

Switch the stand mixer to the paddle attachment. Add the completely cooled meringue back into the stand mixer and turn it on to medium-high speed. Add in small chunks of butter, 1 tablespoon (14 g) at a time, and beat for 15 minutes. The mixture may start to look curdled. Just keep mixing and it will smooth out. Add the vanilla and mix for 1 more minute.

This buttercream can be made ahead of time and stored in the refrigerator. Simply take it out, allow to come to room temperature and rewhip it.

CHOCOLATE GANACHE FILLING: In a medium bowl, add the chocolate chips and set them aside. In a microwave-safe measuring cup, heat the heavy cream in four 15-second intervals, until the temperature reaches 180°F (82°C). Pour it over the chocolate and cover the bowl with plastic wrap for 10 minutes. After it has sat, stir until all the chocolate is melted through. If chunks of chocolate still remain, microwave in 10-second intervals, until smooth. Set the ganache aside to firm up.

RICE CEREAL TREATS: In a medium sauce pot on medium heat, melt the butter and marshmallows. Remove the pan from the heat and mix in the rice cereal until combined. Dump the mixture out on a parchment-lined dinner plate to firm up for 20 to 30 minutes.

MODELING CHOCOLATE: Though cup measurements are provided, it is highly advised that these ingredients be measured by weight. In a heatproof bowl, add the white chocolate candy wafers. Microwave and stir them in 30-second intervals, until they have melted. Set it aside.

Add the corn syrup to a separate small bowl and microwave for 7 seconds—do not exceed 7 seconds or the syrup will burn. Pour the corn syrup into the chocolate and gently fold it in with a rubber spatula until a lumpy dough begins to form. Avoid overmixing because the mixture will start to leach out grease.

Transfer the chocolate dough onto a plastic wrap–lined plate, cover with plastic wrap and push it down into a disk. Let the mixture cool for 45 minutes to 1 hour, until it firms up.

fig. 1 *fig. 2*

ASSEMBLY: With a cake leveler, trim the top of each cake. Set aside the excess cake trimmings in a bowl for later. Add a small dollop of buttercream to the center of a round cake board and add the first cake layer. Fill a piping bag with the chocolate ganache and pipe a border around the top edge of the cake layer about ¼ inch (6 mm) thick. Continue to pipe in a spiral motion from the outside edge to the center. Spread it flat with an offset spatula. Stack the next layer and repeat until all layers are stacked. Crumb coat the cake with a thin layer of buttercream and place it in the freezer for 20 minutes.

Cut a half moon–shaped notch out of the top edge of the cake to prepare the mouth (fig. 1). Sculpt rice cereal treats inside the notch and over the top, creating an arch to act as the top of the mouth (fig. 2). Temporarily use a toothpick to hold the mouth up while sculpting as the treats tend to droop before buttercream is added. Sticking the cake in the freezer for a few minutes to help harden the cereal treats makes them more manageable to work with.

Once the mouth structure is built and the cake is chilled, spread white buttercream on the sides and top to blend the mouth in with the rest of the cake. Really take your time here to make sure that everything looks uniform, including the rim of the cake's mouth. Avoid getting buttercream inside the mouth.

With a paintbrush, stipple chocolate ganache inside the mouth. Break apart the excess cake trimmings from earlier into crumbs and carefully stick them inside the mouth to create the illusion of the inside of the cake. Let it chill in the refrigerator while preparing the modeling chocolate elements.

(continued)

DEVIL'S FOOD CAKE *continued*

DECORATION: Knead the modeling chocolate on a cold surface until it is smooth and workable. Color a handful of each of the following colors to make the mouth elements. It is best to wear gloves to avoid colorful hands. These parts are open to creative interpretation.

    ☞ **Gums (blackish purple):** Roll two long, thin snakes and apply them with gentle pressure on the inside of the top and bottom rim of the mouth.

    ☞ **Tongue (burgundy/red):** Sculpt your version of a tongue to a size that fits inside the mouth. Dab it with a paper towel to create texture. Optionally, paint some highlights and lowlights with oil-based food dye. Place the tongue inside the mouth.

    ☞ **Teeth (off white, a small dab of yellow and brown):** Sculpt sharp teeth. Refer to the photo for sizing variations. Place the teeth on a parchment-lined plate in the freezer to firm up before adding to the mouth. Pre-poke a hole in the gums with a toothpick before applying the teeth.

If the modeling chocolate gets too soft while working, pop it in the freezer for 3 to 5 minutes to firm up again. Once the mouth has all its peculiarities added to it, begin piping.

PIPING: Pipe the details on and around the cake to give it a grand look. The tips that are used are Wilton star tips #16, #18 and #32 and ruffle tip #70. This can also be left to your creative interpretation. The main technique that is applied throughout the cake is called a shell pattern (page 49). The shell pattern technique is done around the base and top of the cake as well as under the mouth.

For the base, pipe a shell pattern all the way around with the larger star tip (Wilton #32). Add a smaller star tip (Wilton #16) shell pattern directly on top of the large one. Do a similar pattern around the top and mouth. The small piping tip (Wilton #16) will cover up any imperfections to make the mouth look like it is seamlessly attached to the cake. Using the medium star tip (Wilton #18), pipe single stars all over the top of the cake. See the star technique on page 49.

Finishing the piping with a nice ruffle around the sides adds grandeur to the cake. Simply measure and mark with a toothpick where you want the swag ruffles to hang. This ensures that each swag will look similar. Attach the ruffle tip #70 to a piping bag. Following the lines, gently squeeze with constant pressure, adding ruffles to the sides of the cake. Add any additional embellishments to your liking. Refrigerate the cake for 30 minutes to firm up. Top with bright red maraschino cherries and BAM! Perfect Devil's Food Cake.

Since this cake contains dairy, it can be left out for a maximum of 4 hours at moderate room temperature. Store leftovers in the refrigerator. Let it thaw completely before eating for the best texture.

    ☞ *Modeling chocolate is shelf stable. Any leftovers can be wrapped and stored in a cool, dry place. For future projects, it will harden as it sits. Re-kneading it will make it workable again.*

FUNERAL-FETTI CAKE

A CAKE OF CONFETTI THAT'S SHROUDED IN BLACK, THIS OMEN OF FATE IS A CURIOUS SNACK. BEFORE YOU CONSUME, YOU SIMPLY MUST KNOW IT'S CURSED WITH VANILLA, COCOA AND WOE.

Yield: 1 (14-inch [35-cm]) cake

....

Heavy-duty aluminum foil

7½ graham crackers

COFFIN PAN: This pan is made with two simple components: heavy-duty aluminum foil and graham crackers. Lay a 41-inch (103-cm)-long piece of heavy-duty aluminum foil on the table. Place the graham crackers in a line 1 inch (2.5 cm) from the bottom of the foil lengthwise, ending with the half cracker at the end. Leave about ⅛ inch (3 mm) between. Fold the bottom half of the foil up on the graham crackers, then fold the sides over to envelop both ends (fig. 1). Finally, fold the top half of the foil down onto the graham crackers, then keep folding it over on itself until you're left with a long aluminum strip. Be gentle so the crackers don't break.

Carefully bend the strip where there are gaps between the crackers and shape it into a coffin (fig. 2). Be sure not to break any of the graham crackers. Place the coffin on a sheet of foil and wrap the overhang inward to secure the walls shut (fig. 3). Place the coffin on a baking tray and spray it with nonstick baking spray. Set it aside until needed.

Preheat the oven to 325°F (165°C).

(continued)

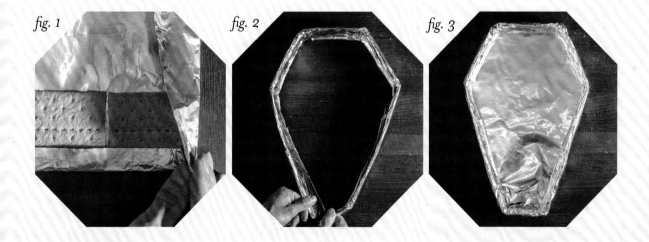

fig. 1   fig. 2   fig. 3

Cake

3 cups (375 g) all-purpose flour

1½ tsp (7 g) baking powder

½ tsp baking soda

1 tsp kosher salt

1 cup (240 g) full-fat sour cream

½ cup (110 g) whole milk

1 cup (226 g/2 sticks) unsalted butter, softened

2 cups (400 g) granulated sugar

2 tbsp (30 g) vanilla extract

6 large eggs, room temperature

½ cup (95 g) black sprinkles (jimmies)

Black Buttercream

¾ cup (150 g) granulated sugar

3 tbsp (30 g) cornstarch

¼ tsp salt

1¼ cups (270 g) whole milk

1 tsp vanilla extract

1 cup (226 g/2 sticks) unsalted butter, softened

4 drops black food dye

⅓ cup (37 g) black cocoa powder

1 tbsp (5 g) Dutch-processed cocoa powder

½ tsp vanilla extract

Special Tools

Cake board

Cookie cutter

Piping bags

Round piping tip (Wilton #3)

Star piping tips (Wilton #18, #16, #1M)

CAKE: In a medium bowl, whisk together the flour, baking powder, baking soda and salt. Set it aside. In a cup, combine the sour cream and milk and set aside.

In a large bowl, use an electric mixer to combine the butter and sugar and beat until creamy, 5 to 7 minutes. Add the vanilla and eggs and mix until combined. With the mixer on its lowest speed, add half of the dry ingredients and half of the sour cream mixture, then mix just until no visible flour remains. Add the remaining dry ingredients and sour cream mixture. Continue to beat the batter for a few seconds, until just combined. Do not overmix; the batter should have some lumps. Fold in the black sprinkles with a rubber spatula.

Pour the batter into the coffin pan and bake for 45-50 minutes on the middle rack. It is done when a toothpick inserted in the middle comes out mostly clean with a bit of crumbs. Allow to cool completely.

BLACK BUTTERCREAM: In a medium saucepan, whisk together the sugar, cornstarch and salt. Add the milk and vanilla and stir to combine. Over medium heat, stir the mixture constantly with a rubber spatula until it thickens into a pudding-like consistency. Remove it from the heat and spread the mixture in a thin layer on a large dinner plate. Cover with plastic wrap, making sure it touches the surface. Let it cool to room temperature until the mixture is congealed, about 45 minutes.

This next part can be done with a hand or stand mixer, but using a stand mixer will cut the time in half. Beat the butter until fluffy, about 3 minutes. With the mixer still running, add the congealed mixture into the butter one spoonful at a time, making sure to beat well after each addition. Once all the congealed mixture is added, beat for 5 more minutes, until creamy and no jelly bits remain.

☞ *The congealed mixture must be completely cooled before adding it to the butter and the butter mustn't be too soft. If the butter is too soft, the cream will become soupy.*

Mix in the black food dye, sift in both cocoa powders and add the vanilla. Use a handheld immersion blender to deepen the color to a true black color. See Conjuring Color (page 172) for more details on this magical method. Add the buttercream to a piping bag.

(continued)

FUNERAL-FETTI CAKE *continued*

ASSEMBLY: Piping takes practice. The design of this cake is customizable to your personal preference and skillset.

Remove the cake from the pan by disassembling the graham cracker sides. Place the cake on a cake board and coat the cake with black buttercream. Mark a circle in the upper center of the coffin with a cookie cutter. Lightly score diamond-shaped gridlines across the cake with a skewer, avoiding the center of the marked circle. Pipe over the gridlines with a round piping tip (Wilton #3). For the base, top edges and around the middle circle, use a star tip (Wilton #18) to pipe a shell pattern (page 49). Pre-mark and measure swags on the side of the cake. Use a star tip (Wilton #16) to pipe a spiral chain by touching the tip to the cake at a 45-degree angle. Gently squeeze the bag and move in a circular motion following the marked lines. Use your non-dominant hand to guide the bag. Lastly, pipe a rosette (page 49) in the middle of the circle with a star piping tip (Wilton #1M). Hold the tip parallel with the cake and pipe in an overlapping circular motion.

Enjoy this dense and somber cake with a glass of milk. Store any leftovers in the refrigerator for 2 to 3 days. Thaw before eating.

Spinach Banana Moss Cake

This mossy slice of woodland dreams is so much more than what it seems.

Yield: 1 (7-inch [18-cm]) four-layer cake

....

Modeling Chocolate Mushrooms
1 (12-oz [350-g]) bag white melting chocolate candy wafers

¼ cup (84 g) light corn syrup

Gel food dye (yellow, brown, green)

Cocoa powder, for brushing

The Pans
Heavy-duty aluminum foil

8 graham crackers

Though the components of this cake are quite strange, know that the spinach is tasteless and only adds a bright green hue to the cake. Fresh baby spinach is used because it has a milder taste compared to adult spinach. The dominant flavors in this cake are banana and chocolate.

MODELING CHOCOLATE: Though cup measurements are provided, it is highly advised that these ingredients be measured by weight. In a heatproof bowl, add the white chocolate candy wafers. Microwave and stir in 30-second intervals, until the chocolate has melted. Set it aside.

Add the corn syrup to a separate small bowl and microwave for 7 seconds—do not exceed 7 seconds or the syrup will burn. Pour the corn syrup into the chocolate and gently fold it in with a rubber spatula until a lumpy dough begins to form. Avoid overmixing because the mixture will start to leach out grease.

Transfer the chocolate onto a plastic wrap–lined plate, cover with plastic wrap and push it down onto a disk. Let the mixture cool for 45 minutes to 1 hour, until it firms up.

THE PANS: The two triangular pans for this cake are easily made with heavy-duty aluminum foil and a few graham crackers. Each pan requires 4 graham crackers. For the first pan, lay a 24-inch (60-cm)-long piece of heavy-duty aluminum foil on the table. Break 1 whole graham cracker in half down the score mark and leave the other 3 as they are. Place the graham crackers in a line 1 inch (2.5 cm) from the bottom of the foil lengthwise in this order: whole, half, whole, whole, half. Leave about ⅛ inch (3 mm) between them. Fold the bottom half up on the graham crackers, then fold the sides over to envelope both ends (fig. 1). Fold the top half of the foil down onto the graham crackers, then keep folding it over on itself until you're left with a long aluminum strip. Be gentle so the crackers don't break.

(continued)

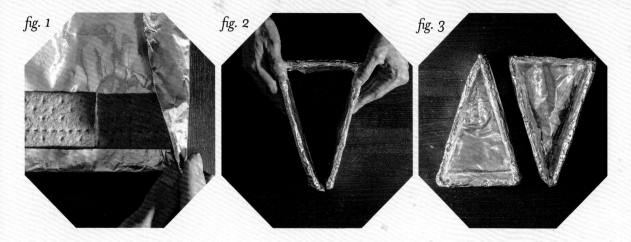

fig. 1 *fig. 2* *fig. 3*

SPINACH BANANA MOSS CAKE *continued*

Spinach Cake

1½ cups (188 g) all-purpose flour

1 tsp baking powder

1 tsp baking soda

¼ tsp salt

½ cup (100 g) baby spinach, blanched

½ cup (120 g) whole milk

1 tbsp (15 g) white vinegar

½ cup (113 g/1 stick) unsalted butter, softened

½ cup (100 g) granulated sugar

¼ cup (55 g) dark brown sugar

1 large egg

1 tsp vanilla extract

⅔ cup (185 g) ripe mashed bananas (about 2½ bananas)

Carefully bend the strip where there are gaps between the crackers and shape it into a triangle (fig. 2). Add a larger piece of foil on the bottom and fold it over the outside to secure the pan closed. Smooth the inside as much as possible without putting too much pressure on the crackers. Repeat to make a second pan (fig. 3). Spray them with nonstick baking spray and place them on a baking tray. Set aside.

Preheat the oven to 325°F (165°C).

SPINACH CAKE: In a medium bowl, whisk together the flour, baking powder, baking soda and salt. Set it aside.

To blanch the spinach, bring a medium pot of water to a roaring boil. In small batches, add the spinach and let it swim for 10 seconds for the leaves to wilt. Fish them out with a slotted spoon. Repeat until all the spinach has been wilted. Squeeze some of the excess liquid out of the spinach before adding it to a blender with the milk. Obliterate for 2 minutes, until smooth. Transfer it to a glass measuring cup, stir in the white vinegar and set it aside. This will begin to curdle and separate into a green sludge. This acidic mixture will help the cake rise. Trust the process.

In a large bowl, beat the butter and both sugars until fluffy, about 3 minutes. Add the egg and vanilla and mix for 30 more seconds, until incorporated. Add the mashed bananas and spinach mixture and beat for another minute. Sift in the dry ingredients and fold it in by hand with a rubber spatula just until there are no more visible streaks of flour. Do not overmix; the batter should be lumpy. Working with haste, separate the batter evenly between both triangle pans.

(continued)

SPINACH BANANA MOSS CAKE *continued*

Cookie Dirt

10 Oreo® cookies

1½ tbsp (6 g) almond flour or white cookies (see Note)

Chocolate Buttercream

¾ cup (150 g) granulated sugar

3 tbsp (30 g) cornstarch

¼ tsp salt

1¼ cups (270 g) whole milk

1 tsp vanilla extract

1 cup (226 g/2 sticks) unsalted butter, softened

1 tbsp (5 g) cocoa powder

3 drops brown food dye

Bake at 325°F (165°C) for 40 to 45 minutes, until a toothpick inserted in the center comes out mostly clean. Let the cakes cool inside the pans.

COOKIE DIRT: Remove the cream and crush the Oreo cookies into fine crumbs with a food processor or by hand. Measure ⅔ cup (80 g) of Oreo cookie crumbs and add the almond flour to create fake dirt.

☛ *The cookie dirt can be made nut-free by substituting almond flour for a ground white cookie of your liking. Separate ⅓ cup (43 g) and set it aside for the chocolate buttercream.*

CHOCOLATE BUTTERCREAM: In a medium saucepan, whisk together the sugar, cornstarch and salt. Add the milk and vanilla and stir to combine. Over medium heat, stir the mixture constantly with a rubber spatula until it thickens into a pudding-like consistency. Remove it from the heat and spread the mixture in a thin layer on a large dinner plate. Cover with plastic wrap, making sure it touches the surface. Let it cool to room temperature until it congeals.

This next step can be done with a hand or stand mixer, but using a stand mixer will cut the time in half. Beat the butter until fluffy, about 3 minutes. With the mixer still running, spoon the congealed mixture into the butter one spoonful at a time, making sure to beat well after each addition. Once all the mixture is added, beat for 5 more minutes, until creamy and no jelly bits remain. Beat in the reserved cookie dirt, cocoa powder and brown food dye until combined. If the buttercream is too soft, place it in the refrigerator for 30 minutes, making sure to stir it every 10 minutes, until it is of frosting consistency. Add it to a piping bag.

ASSEMBLY: Remove the cakes from their pans by disassembling the sides. With a serrated knife, trim the sides, back and top of the cakes to even it out. The cutoff will be used for the moss topping later, so put it in a bowl and set aside. Cut each cake into two even layers using a cake leveler. Place the first triangle cake layer on your desired plate and pipe a layer of buttercream on top. Make sure it isn't too thick. Repeat the process for the remaining layers. A bit of the cream should ooze out of the sides because of the weight of the cake. Scoop the cookie dirt into a spoon and hold it up against a cream layer. Push the dirt onto the cream until it is completely covered. Repeat for each cream layer. Refrigerate for 30 minutes to set. After it has set, apply buttercream on the top and back of the cake. Add cookie dirt until there is no visible cream. Break up the excess cake pieces into small crumbs and add them to the top and back of the cake to create a moss effect.

MUSHROOMS: Knead the modeling chocolate on a cold surface until it is smooth and workable. Color half of the modeling chocolate with gel food dye to make a mushroom hue. A small amount of yellow, brown and green will do. Sculpt the stem on a toothpick and attach the cap. Use a dry paintbrush to dust the bottom of the mushroom with cocoa powder. Lightly brush the outside to give it some depth. Add them to the cake, and BAM! A perfect slice of nature.

Store any leftovers in the refrigerator covered for 2 to 3 days. Let the cake come to room temperature before eating to give the buttercream time to thaw.

☞ *Modeling chocolate is shelf stable. Any leftovers can be wrapped and stored in a cool, dry place. For future projects, it will harden as it sits. Re-kneading it will make it workable again.*

Tarot Sun Sheet Cake

A sweet little fortune found in the cards! Spongy and light, it's all in good fun. Coconut and pineapple send their regards, beaming bright like the summer sun.

Yield: 1 (9 x 13-inch [23 x 33-cm]) sheet cake

Pineapple Curd

2 large egg whites

2 large egg yolks

¼ cup (50 g) granulated sugar

2 tbsp (20 g) cornstarch

1 cup (200 g) canned 100% pineapple juice

⅛ tsp kosher salt

2 tbsp (28 g) cold unsalted butter, cubed

Coconut Cake

3 cups (375 g) all-purpose flour

1½ tsp (7 g) baking powder

½ tsp baking soda

1 tsp kosher salt

1 (13.5-oz [383-g]) can full-fat coconut milk

2 tbsp (30 g) white vinegar

1 cup (226 g/2 sticks) unsalted butter, softened

2 cups (400 g) granulated sugar

6 eggs, room temperature

1 tbsp (14 g) vanilla extract

½ cup (47 g) unsweetened shredded coconut

PINEAPPLE CURD: Prepare a double boiler by adding 1 inch (2.5 cm) of water to a small sauce pot. Let the water simmer on medium heat. To a heatproof bowl big enough to sit on the rim of the pot, add the egg whites, egg yolks, sugar and cornstarch and whisk until combined. Add the pineapple juice and salt and whisk until incorporated. Rest the bowl on top of the rim of the simmering pot. Stir the mixture constantly with a whisk until it thickens to the consistency of pudding and the temperature reads 175°F (79°C). This will take 12 to 15 minutes. It will seem like nothing is happening at first, but it will thicken up eventually. Immediately remove it from the heat and stir in the cold butter and let it melt. Run the curd through a fine-mesh sieve into a clean bowl to remove any clumps. Remember to scrape off the curd that gathers at the bottom of the sieve. Cover the surface with plastic wrap to prevent skin from forming. Refrigerate for at least 1 hour, or until it is set.

COCONUT CAKE: Preheat the oven to 375°F (190°C) and spray a 9 x 13–inch (23 x 33–cm) cake pan with nonstick baking spray.

In a medium bowl, whisk together the flour, baking powder, baking soda and salt and set it aside. In a cup, combine the coconut milk and vinegar and set it aside.

In a large bowl, combine the butter and sugar. Beat until fluffy with an electric mixer for 3 minutes. Add the eggs and vanilla and beat until combined. Add half the dry mixture, then half the coconut milk mixture and beat on low speed until just incorporated. Repeat with the remaining dry ingredients and coconut milk mixture. Increase the speed to medium and continue to beat the batter for another 30 seconds. Gently fold in the shredded coconut and pour the batter into the greased cake pan. Bake it for 23 to 25 minutes, until the edges are beginning to brown and a toothpick inserted in the center comes out clean.

(continued)

TAROT SUN SHEET CAKE *continued*

Buttercream

¾ cup (150 g) granulated sugar

3 tbsp (30 g) cornstarch

¼ tsp salt

1¼ cups (270 g) whole milk

1 tsp vanilla extract

1 cup (226 g/2 sticks) unsalted butter, softened

Gel food dye (yellow, orange, black, purple, off-white)

Special Tools

9 x 13–inch (23 x 33–cm) cake pan

Sun Tarot template (page 177)

Clear tape

White parchment paper

Piping bags

Cake leveler or serrated knife

Pour the batter into the greased cake pan and bake for 23 to 25 minutes, until the edges are beginning to brown and a toothpick inserted in the center comes out clean. Cool completely in the pan.

BUTTERCREAM: In a medium saucepan, whisk together the sugar, cornstarch and salt. Add the milk and vanilla and stir to combine. Over medium heat, stir the mixture constantly with a rubber spatula until it thickens into a pudding-like consistency. Remove it from the heat and spread the mixture in a thin layer on a large dinner plate. Cover with plastic wrap, making sure it touches the surface. Let it sit at room temperature for about 45 minutes, until it has cooled completely and congealed.

This next part can be done with a hand or stand mixer, but a stand mixer will cut the time in half. Beat the butter for 3 minutes, until fluffy. With the mixer still running, add the congealed mixture into the butter one spoonful at a time, making sure to beat well after each addition. Once all the mixture has been added, beat for 5 more minutes, until creamy and no jelly bits remain.

☞ *The congealed mixture must be completely cooled before adding it to the butter, and the butter must be soft but not too soft. If the butter is too soft, the cream will become soupy.*

To get vibrant colors in buttercream, it is best to enhance them with an immersion blender (see Conjuring Color [page 172]). The blender step is optional, but the colors will lack vibrancy if not done. It is not advised to add more dye than listed, or the taste of the cream will be severely altered.

Separate and color the buttercream as follows:

☞ 1 cup (200 g) purple

☞ ¾ cup (150 g) off-white

☞ ½ cup (100 g) yellow

☞ ¼ cup (50 g) black

After the sun's face is filled in with yellow buttercream, halve the remaining buttercream and mix a drop or two of orange food dye into the leftover yellow buttercream for the sun's rays. Alternate between yellow and orange to add dimension.

fig. 1

fig. 2

SUN BUTTERCREAM TRANSFER: Tape the template together and cut it out along the border. Tape it to the back of a baking tray. Place a flat piece of parchment paper on top of the template and tape it down on all four sides to secure it. The template should show through the parchment paper to use as a guide.

With the black buttercream in a piping bag, snip the tip as small as the lines on the template. Trace the black lines of the template with the black buttercream. Use a toothpick to get the thin lines such as the lettering and cloud details. Place the baking sheet in the freezer for 7 minutes to stiffen the buttercream. Add the yellow and orange to the sun and its rays and freeze for 7 more minutes. Continue this with the off-white and purple buttercream, freezing for 7 minutes in between each color. Use the pictures as a guide. After the last freezing, use any leftover colored buttercream to level out the backside (it won't be seen). Let the design harden in the freezer for 1 hour (fig. 1).

ASSEMBLY: Turn out the cooled cake onto a cutting board. Use a cake leveler or serrated knife to saw the cake into two layers lengthwise. It will feel a bit tough because of the coconut shreds inside. Place the top layer of the cake back into the pan upside down. Dump and spread the pineapple curd onto it. Place the bottom layer of cake back into the pan with the flat side facing up. Remove the buttercream tarot card from the freezer and carefully turn it over onto the cake. Slowly peel back the parchment paper to reveal the image (fig. 2). Let the buttercream come to room temperature to adhere to the cake before slicing. And BAM! Perfect Tarot Sun Sheet Cake.

Store in the refrigerator covered for up to 3 days.

Pumpkin Caramel Fortune Cake

Yield: 1 (8-inch [20-cm]) four-layer cake

....

Caramel Cream Filling

4 oz (113 g) cream cheese, softened

3 tbsp (62 g) caramel sauce

A GAME OF FORTUNE:

This is a 1920s-era game that was played by young adults at Halloween parties. The host would stick charms in the cake before decorating it, and each guest would take a slice to receive their fortune. These charms were symbols of fate. To prepare your charms for the cake, thoroughly clean them with soap and water. Wrap them in aluminum foil the size of a small bouncy ball, about 1 inch (2.5 cm).

☛ *IMPORTANT: Adding charms to your cake can be fun, but please proceed with caution. It is advised that the host informs all who participate in the fortune cake of potential (non-edible) charms in each piece. It's best to make sure all the cake is sifted through and all the charms are accounted for before having everyone eat the cake. It is also advised that this game be played by* **adults only.**

☛ **Ring:** You will be engaged or married within a year.

☛ **Button:** You will find disappointment in love.

☛ **Thimble:** You will become unmarried or a spinster in the coming year.

☛ **Key:** You will embark on an early journey.

☛ **Penny:** You will obtain wealth within the coming year.

CARAMEL CREAM FILLING: Whisk together the cream cheese and caramel sauce until combined. Add it to a piping bag and set it aside.

Preheat the oven to 325°F (165°C). Grease two 8-inch (20-cm) round cake pans with baking spray.

(continued)

PUMPKIN CARAMEL FORTUNE CAKE *continued*

Moist Pumpkin Cake

1 can (15 oz) pumpkin puree

3 cups (375 g) all-purpose flour

1½ tsp (10 g) baking soda

½ tsp baking powder

½ tsp kosher salt

2 tbsp (13 g) pumpkin pie spice

¾ cup (170 g) unsalted butter

1 cup (200 g) granulated sugar

½ cup (110 g) dark brown sugar

3 large eggs, room temperature

2½ tsp (12 g) vanilla extract

¼ cup (56 g) vegetable oil

½ cup (120 g) sour cream

½ cup (113 g) water

1½ tsp (7 g) vinegar

Buttercream

1½ cups (300 g) granulated sugar

6 tbsp (48 g) cornstarch

½ tsp kosher salt

2½ cups (590 g) whole milk

2 tsp (8 g) vanilla extract

2 cups (454 g) unsalted butter, softened

Gel food dye (black, orange, blue)

1 tbsp (7 g) black cocoa powder

Special Tools

Charms: ring, thimble, button, key, penny

Two 8-inch (20-cm) round cake pans

Cake leveler or bread knife

Immersion blender

Witch template (page 177)

Piping bags

Star piping tips (Wilton #1M, #21)

MOIST PUMPKIN CAKE: Add the pumpkin puree to a saucepan on medium heat. While stirring constantly, cook it down until the puree reduces to 1¼ cups (295g). This should take about 8-10 minutes. Once reduced, add it to a bowl and place it in the refrigerator until ready to use.

In a medium bowl sift together the flour, baking soda, baking powder, salt and pumpkin pie spice. Set it aside. In a large bowl beat the butter and both sugars for 3 minutes until fluffy. Beat in the eggs, one at a time, just until incorporated. Add in the vanilla extract and cooled pumpkin puree and beat until combined. Pour in the oil and beat just until the batter looks uniform.

In a glass measuring cup, combine the sour cream with the water and vinegar. Add half of the dry ingredients and half of the sour cream mixture into the pumpkin batter and fold it in slowly until just combined making sure not to overmix. Add the second half of the dry mixture and sour cream and fold it in for about 15 folds just until there are no more streaks of flour left. The batter will be thick. Divide the batter evenly between the cake pans. Flatten the batter with an offset spatula. Tap the bottoms on the counter to help release any air bubbles. Bake for 35-40 minutes until a toothpick inserted in the center comes out with a bit of crumbs on it. Let the cake cool for 15 minutes then dump it on a baking rack to cool completely. Meanwhile prepare the buttercream.

BUTTERCREAM: In a medium saucepan, whisk together the sugar, cornstarch and salt. Add the milk and vanilla and stir to combine. Over medium heat, stir the mixture constantly with a rubber spatula until it thickens into a pudding-like consistency. Remove the saucepan from the heat and spread the mixture in a thin layer on a large dinner plate. Cover with plastic wrap, making sure it touches the surface. Let it sit at room temperature for about 45 minutes, until it has cooled completely and congealed.

This next part can be done with a hand or stand mixer, but a stand mixer will cut the time in half. Beat the butter for 3 minutes, until fluffy. With the mixer still running, spoon the congealed mixture into the butter one spoonful at a time, making sure to beat well after each addition. Once all the mixture is added, beat for 5 more minutes, until creamy and no jelly bits remain.

☞ *The congealed mixture must be completely cooled before adding it to the butter, and the butter must be soft but not too soft. If the butter is too soft, the cream will become soupy.*

To get vibrant colors in buttercream, it is best to enhance it with an immersion blender. (See Conjuring Color [page 172] for the explanation.) The blender step is optional, but the colors will lack vibrancy if not done. It is not advised to add more dye than listed, or the taste of the cream will be altered severely.

Divide and color the buttercream in separate bowls as follows:

☞ **Black:** 1 cup (200 g) buttercream + 3 drops black food dye + 1 tbsp (7 g) black cocoa powder

☞ **Aged Orange:** 1 cup (200 g) buttercream + 4 drops orange food dye + the teeniest amount of blue food dye, as small as the tip of a toothpick

☞ **White:** ¼ cup (50 g) buttercream, no dye needed

☞ **Light Orange:** Remaining buttercream + 5 drops orange food dye + smallest amount of blue food dye. **Do not enhance with the immersion blender.**

Once the buttercreams have been enhanced with the immersion blender (except for the light orange buttercream), they tend to get a bit softer, which is the perfect consistency for the buttercream witch transfer.

ASSEMBLY: Trim the dome off the cakes to level them out using a cake leveler or bread knife. Cut each layer in half lengthwise to get four total layers. Place the first layer on a cake stand and spread ⅓ cup (70 g) of light orange buttercream on top. This layer will be thin. Avoid adding more to make sure there is enough buttercream for the decorative piping at the end. Pipe a third of the caramel cream filling in a spiral on top of the buttercream layer and spread it flat. Repeat the process until all the cakes are stacked and leveled. If you choose to add charms, wrap them in foil so they are the size of a small bouncy ball (about 1 inch [2.5 cm]). Stick them into the cake, then crumb coat the cake with light orange buttercream. Refrigerate the cake for 30 minutes.

Once the cake has chilled, continue to frost the cake, making sure to be mindful of how much buttercream is used. The less buttercream used on this step means there will be a lot more to decorate with in the end. Place the cake in the fridge while you prepare the buttercream transfer.

BUTTERCREAM WITCH TRANSFER: Print out the witch template and tape it to the back of a baking tray. Place a piece of flat parchment paper on top and tape it on all four sides to prevent it from moving. The tape won't stick to the parchment paper but should hold it in place like a frame. Starting with the black buttercream, add half of it to a piping bag and cut the tip as small as the lines of the drawing. Trace the black lines and fill in the black spaces of the template. Use a toothpick to help with the thinner lines such as the witches face, stars and moon details. Place it in the freezer for 7 minutes. Fill the white spaces with the white buttercream, then freeze for 7 minutes. Lastly, fill in the orange spaces with the aged orange buttercream and freeze for another 7 minutes. Pipe light orange buttercream all over the back side of the transfer and level it out to lock everything in place (it won't be seen). Let the witch harden in the freezer for 1 hour.

(continued)

PUMPKIN CARAMEL FORTUNE CAKE
continued

DECORATING: Working quickly, apply the witch buttercream transfer onto the cake by flipping it over on the center. Slowly peel the parchment paper off. Use light orange buttercream to fill in any gaps between the witch and the top of the cake.

Mix the leftover light orange buttercream with the aged orange buttercream. Adjust the color by adding 1 to 2 drops of orange food dye to get a larger batch of dark orange. Hit it with the immersion blender again to enhance the color.

Using the dark orange buttercream, pipe a shell pattern (page 49) with a large star tip (Wilton #1M) around the top and sides of the cake. Add a (Wilton #21) star tip to a piping bag with black buttercream. Pipe little stars around the sides of the cake by holding the piping bag parallel to the side of the cake. Give the bag a little squeeze and pull it away.

Because this cake contains dairy, any leftovers must be refrigerated. Store it in the fridge for 2 to 3 days. Let it sit on the counter for 1 hour after removing it from the refrigerator to come to room temperature.

ZEBRA-SPIDER CHEESECAKE

Yield: 1 (8½-inch [21-cm]) *cheesecake*

....

THIS DECADENT WEB, AN EYEFUL OF FRIGHT, HAS MARBLES OF CHOCOLATE BLACK AS THE NIGHT. THIS VISUAL FEAST, A MARVELOUS SIGHT, HOLDS PROMISE TO MAKE THE TASTE BUDS IGNITE.

Cookie Crust

30 Oreos, pulsed into crumbs

3 tbsp (39 g) granulated sugar

1 tbsp (7 g) black cocoa powder, sifted

7 tbsp (98 g) unsalted butter, melted

Cheesecake Filling

4 (8-oz [227-g]) cream cheese blocks, softened

1½ cups (300 g) granulated sugar

3 tbsp (30 g) cornstarch

1 tbsp (13 g) vanilla extract

1 tsp lemon juice

4 large eggs, room temperature

¾ cup (173 g) full-fat sour cream, room temperature

½ cup (100 g) heavy cream, room temperature

2 tbsp (14 g) black cocoa powder, sifted

Special Tools

8½-inch (21-cm) springform pan

Oven bag

Bakers' twine

Deep casserole dish

Bring all the ingredients up to room temperature before proceeding to avoid clumping. Preheat the oven to 350°F (180°C). Lightly coat an 8½-inch (21-cm) springform pan with baking spray.

COOKIE CRUST: In a bowl, combine the finely crushed Oreos, sugar, black cocoa power and melted butter. Mix with a fork until the texture becomes like wet sand. Pour three-quarters of the mixture into the prepared springform pan. Evenly press the crumbs against the walls of the pan about three-quarters of the way up. Use the bottom of a measuring cup to pack the crumbs in firmly. Add the rest of the crumbs and press them into the bottom of the pan.

Bake for 7 to 10 minutes, then let it cool completely. Meanwhile, prepare the filling.

CHEESECAKE FILLING: Lower the oven temperature to 305°F (150°C). In a large bowl, whisk the cream cheese, sugar, cornstarch, vanilla and lemon juice until smooth, about 30 seconds. Switch to a rubber spatula and add the eggs, one at a time, mixing slowly and thoroughly after each addition. Keep in mind that using a whisk or mixing vigorously at this point is not advised. It will incorporate too many air bubbles into the mixture, which will make the final product less attractive.

In a small cup, mix the sour cream and heavy cream. Gently fold it into the batter. Divide the batter evenly between two large mixing bowls. Sift the black cocoa powder into one bowl and gently mix, just until thoroughly uniform in color, while trying not to overmix the batter.

(continued)

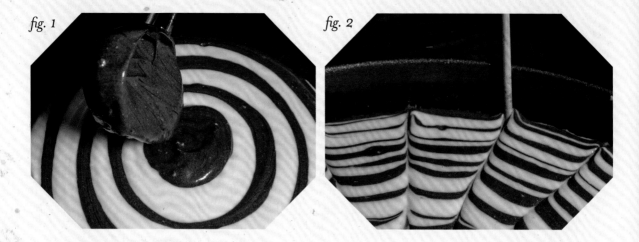

fig. 1   fig. 2

ZEBRA-SPIDER CHEESECAKE *continued*

Add the batter, about ¼ cup (50 g) at a time, to the center of the cooled cookie crust. Alternate the colors until all the batter is used up. Slightly shake the pan to even the batter out. Gradually use less batter as the rings begin to form into a target. As an option, add the batter to piping bags to get cleaner rounds on the cake. This option is messier to work with but yields a great result. Run a toothpick from the center of the cheesecake out to the edge to create a spiderweb pattern.

BAIN-MARIE: Boil a kettle of water. Open the oven bag and cut it in half to make it smaller. Carefully place the cheesecake inside and tie bakers' twine around the rim of the pan to secure the bag to it. Fold the excess plastic down the sides of the pan. Securely cover the bottom and sides of the cheesecake pan with three layers of heavy-duty aluminum foil. This helps prevent water from seeping into the crust.

Place a tea towel on the bottom of a deep casserole dish. Make sure that the casserole dish is large enough to accommodate the size of the cheesecake pan. Place the cheesecake pan into the deep casserole dish. Pull the top oven rack out a bit and place the casserole dish with the cheesecake in the oven. Fill the casserole dish with enough boiling water until it reaches about halfway up the sides of the cheesecake pan.

Bake the cheesecake at 305°F (150°C) for 1 hour and 30 to 35 minutes. The cheesecake will have puffed up a bit, and the center will slightly jiggle. At this point, turn off the oven, crack the oven door and leave the cheesecake to cool inside for 1 hour. Slowly cooling the cheesecake in the oven prevents the top from cracking, which happens due to a sudden change in temperature.

After an hour, remove the cheesecake from the water bath and take off the foil and oven bag. Cover the cheesecake with foil and place it in the refrigerator overnight to firm up. The next day, remove the cheesecake from the springform pan by placing it on a food can and sliding the walls of the springform pan down.

This treat is best served cold. To get clean slices, dip the knife in warm water and wipe it before and after each slice. Store covered in the fridge for up to 5 days.

FIGGY STICKY TOFFEE PUDDING

A MODERN TWIST ON A CLASSIC CAKE, IT'S QUITE IMPRESSIVE AND QUICK TO MAKE. STICKY AND GOOEY, A TEXTURE SUBLIME, WITH WARM WINTER SPICES AND FLAVORS DIVINE. AROMA OF FIG AND TOFFEE ENHANCE THE SPIRIT OF YULE WHO OFFERS A TRANCE.

Yield: 8 *puddings*

¾ cup (97 g) finely chopped walnuts

Toffee Sauce

1 cup (235 g) heavy cream

1 cup (220 g) dark brown sugar

½ cup (113 g/1 stick) unsalted butter

¼ tsp kosher salt

1 tsp vanilla extract

Crème Anglaise

¼ cup (50 g) granulated sugar

3 large egg yolks

1 tsp cornstarch

1 cup (235 g) heavy whipping cream

2 tsp (8 g) vanilla extract

Preheat the oven to 350°F (180°C). Spray a jumbo muffin pan with nonstick baking spray. Add the walnuts in an even layer at the bottom of each muffin well.

☞ *This makes 8 jumbo cakes. If you only have a pan with 6 wells, you can bake the last two after the first batch. Set the pan aside.*

TOFFEE SAUCE: Add the heavy cream, brown sugar, butter, salt and vanilla to a medium sauce pot over medium-low heat. Give it a quick stir, then leave it to cook until the butter melts and the mixture begins to bubble. Stir until the sauce begins to thicken slightly and the temperature reaches 220°F (105°C). This is a runny sauce that will thicken up while it cools. Set it aside.

CRÈME ANGLAISE: To make a double boiler, add 1 inch (2.5 cm) of water to a small sauce pot. Bring it to a simmer on low heat. To a heatproof bowl large enough to fit over the simmering pot without touching the water, whisk together the sugar, egg yolks and cornstarch until combined. Whisk in the heavy cream and vanilla until evenly combined. Rest the bowl above the simmering pot. Switch to a rubber spatula and stir constantly until the mixture reaches 165°F (73°C) and coats the back of a spoon. It should leave a track on the back of the spoon when you run a finger through it. Transfer the mixture to another bowl, cover with plastic wrap and place in the refrigerator to cool.

☞ *Though vanilla sauce is recommended, a quick alternative to crème anglaise is vanilla ice cream.*

(continued)

FIGGY STICKY TOFFEE PUDDING *continued*

Fig Cake

1½ cups (250 g) dried figs

1½ cups (188 g) all-purpose flour

1½ tsp (7 g) baking powder

½ tsp baking soda

1 tsp cinnamon

½ tsp ginger

½ tsp nutmeg

½ tsp salt

½ cup (113 g/1 stick) unsalted butter, softened

⅔ cup (158 g) dark brown sugar

3 large eggs

¼ cup (60 g) full-fat sour cream

¼ cup (55 g) milk

2 tbsp (40 g) molasses

2 tsp (8 g) vanilla extract

FIG CAKE: Cut the stems off the dried figs and place them in a small bowl. Pour in just enough boiling water to submerge them. Cover the bowl with a plate for 15 minutes until the figs soften. Once the figs have softened, reserve ¼ cup (59 g) of the water and place it in a blender along with the figs. Blend until smooth, then set it aside.

In a small bowl, whisk together the flour, baking powder, baking soda, cinnamon, ginger, nutmeg and salt until combined. Set it aside.

In a large bowl, beat the softened butter and brown sugar for about 3 minutes, until creamy. Add the eggs and beat for 2 more minutes. Add the blended figs, sour cream, milk, molasses and vanilla and beat for 1 more minute to thoroughly combine. Sift in the dry ingredients and fold it in until just combined and there are no more visible streaks of flour. Do not overmix or the cake will become tough.

Once the batter is mixed, place 2 tablespoons (30 g) of the toffee sauce into the bottom of each muffin tin well. Add the batter with a cookie scoop until the batter reaches three-quarters of the way to the top of the well. Even it out with the back of a spoon.

Bake for 20 to 23 minutes, until a toothpick comes out mostly clean. While the cakes are still warm, dump them out of the pan and place on serving plates. Drizzle with more toffee sauce and the crème anglaise and enjoy. These are best when served warm. These can be made ahead and reheated in the microwave for 5 to 10 seconds before serving. The sauces should be stored in the refrigerator until ready to use.

TEA-RAMISU

Yield: 6 teacups

....

Ladyfingers

½ cup (63 g) all-purpose flour

¼ tsp kosher salt

⅛ tsp baking powder

1 tbsp (10 g) cornstarch

2 eggs, separated

¼ cup + 1 tsp (60 g) granulated sugar, divided

1 tsp vanilla extract

Powdered sugar, for dusting

Tea Concentrate

12 strong tea bags, Earl Grey or chai

1½ cups (330 g) hot water

¼ cup (50 g) granulated sugar

> LIGHT AND ELEGANT,
> STRANGE AND SWEET, ITS
> EARL GREY FLAVOR IS QUITE
> A TREAT. MASCARPONE AND
> COCOA WALTZING SO FINE,
> WHEN SERVED IN A TEACUP
> IT'S TRULY SUBLIME.

Preheat the oven to 355°F (180°C) and line a baking sheet with parchment paper.

LADYFINGERS: In a medium bowl, whisk the flour, salt, baking powder and cornstarch and set it aside.

Separate the egg whites into one mixing bowl and the egg yolks in another. With an electric mixer, beat the egg whites until they are fluffy like sudsy shampoo. Slowly sprinkle in 3 tablespoons (39 g) of granulated sugar, 1 tablespoon (13 g) at a time, until stiff peaks form.

In the other bowl, beat the egg yolks, vanilla and the remaining granulated sugar until fluffy and pale yellow. With a rubber spatula, fold a third of the fluffy egg white mixture into the yolk mixture to loosen the batter. Gently fold in the remaining egg whites.

Sift in the dry ingredients and gently fold until there are no more streaks of flour. Avoid overmixing the batter. Add the batter to a piping bag. On the parchment-lined baking sheet, pipe rounds the size of the middle and bottom diameter of your chosen teacup. (Each teacup will have two ladyfinger biscuits.)

Sift a generous dusting of powdered sugar over the biscuits and bake them for 13 minutes. Remove them from the oven and allow them to cool completely on the baking sheet.

TEA CONCENTRATE: Add the tea bags to a bowl and pour the hot water over them. Cover the bowl with a plate and steep the tea for 5 to 6 minutes. Don't steep the tea for longer than directed on the packaging or the tea will become bitter. Discard the tea bags and stir in the sugar until dissolved. Let it cool.

(continued)

Custard Cream

6 large eggs, separated

½ cup (100 g) granulated sugar, divided

2 tsp (8 g) vanilla extract

¼ tsp kosher salt

16 oz (454 g) mascarpone cheese, room temperature

Cocoa powder, for dusting

Special Tools

Piping bag

6 teacups

Deep casserole dish

Star template (page 177)

CUSTARD CREAM: Have an electric hand mixer handy. Make a double boiler by adding 1 inch (2.5 cm) of water to a small pot and bringing it to a simmer on medium heat. In a medium heatproof bowl, whisk the egg yolks, ¼ cup (50 g) of sugar and vanilla until combined. Set the bowl on top of the double boiler and whisk the yolks until the mixture turns thick and pale yellow. Once the temperature hits 145°F (62°C), remove the bowl from the double boiler and immediately beat the egg yolks with the electric hand mixer for 2 minutes. Scrape the mixture onto a large dinner plate to cool. Wash and dry the same bowl and beater whisks to prepare for the next step.

In a separate heatproof bowl, add the egg whites and the remaining ¼ cup (50 g) of sugar and whisk until incorporated. Place the bowl over the double boiler and whisk constantly until the temperature reaches 145°F (62°C). Immediately remove the bowl from the heat and beat with the electric hand mixer until the mixture comes to room temperature and forms foamy, stiff peaks, 8 to 10 minutes.

In a large bowl, add the room-temperature mascarpone cheese and the cooled egg yolk mixture. Beat with an electric mixer for 30 seconds, just until the ingredients are combined. Fold in a third of the egg white mixture to loosen the batter, then fold in the rest. The mixture will look lumpy at this point. Using an immersion blender or food processor, blitz the mixture until it is smooth. It should be silky and runny.

ASSEMBLY: Spoon a small layer of custard into the teacups. Working one at a time, dunk the smaller round ladyfinger into the tea concentrate for 3 seconds only. Any longer and it will become too soggy. Place it into the teacup. Spoon another thick layer of custard into the teacup, then add the larger round ladyfinger. Top it off with custard and level it out. Lightly tap the teacup on the counter to expel any air bubbles. Repeat for the rest of the teacups.

Place the teacups in a deep casserole dish and cover with a dome of aluminum foil, making sure it doesn't touch the smooth custard tops. Refrigerate them for 2 hours or overnight to set. Before serving, place the star stencil over the top and dust with cocoa powder. Enjoy.

HONEY LAVENDER JAR CAKE

(MEDOVIK CAKE)

ESSENCE OF HONEY, GOLDEN AND PURE. INFUSED WITH LAVENDER'S FRAGRANT ALLURE. SERVED IN A JAR, THIS LUSCIOUS DELIGHT. A MOUTHFUL OF SPRING IN EVERY BITE.

Yield: 6 (8-oz [236-ml]) jar cakes

....

Lavender Milk Soak
½ cup (110 g) whole milk
1 tsp crushed lavender

Honey Biscuit
3 cups (375 g) all-purpose flour
¼ tsp kosher salt
6 tbsp (90 g) unsalted butter
¼ cup (85 g) honey
⅓ cup (67 g) granulated sugar
¾ tsp baking soda
2 large eggs

LAVENDER MILK SOAK: In a small saucepan, bring the milk to a simmer. Remove from the heat and add the crushed lavender. Let it steep for 5 to 8 minutes. Strain the milk through a sieve to remove the lavender buds. Set aside to cool. Save the steeped lavender remains for the cake biscuit.

Preheat the oven to 325°F (165°C).

HONEY BISCUIT: In a medium bowl, whisk together the flour and salt and set it aside. In a tall sauce pot on medium heat, melt the butter. Add the honey and sugar and mix until dissolved. Bring the mixture to a simmer for 1 to 2 minutes. Add the steeped lavender remains and baking soda and whisk immediately. The mixture will bubble up and double in size. Keep mixing until it turns from a light-yellow color to a deep honey color. Take it off the heat and set it aside for 10 minutes to slightly cool.

In a glass measuring cup, lightly whisk the eggs. Add them in a slow, steady stream to the honey mixture while mixing constantly. The color will darken. Avoid dumping the eggs in all at once or they will run the risk of scrambling. Sift in the flour mixture, about 1 cup (125 g) at a time, making sure it is incorporated after each addition. It's best to use a rubber spatula in a folding motion for this part because the dough will thicken.

Once the dough has come together, dump it out on a lightly floured surface and bring it together into a ball, making sure not to knead it. Wrap the dough in plastic wrap and refrigerate it for 20 to 30 minutes to set.

(continued)

Honey Lavender Cake *continued*

Cream

1 cup (235 g) cold heavy whipping cream

⅔ cup (152 g) sour cream

⅔ cup (80 g) powdered sugar

1 tbsp (21 g) honey

A pinch of kosher salt

Honeycomb Topping

Yellow wafer chocolate melts

Brown wafer chocolate melts

Honey, for drizzling (optional; see Note)

Special Tools

8-oz (236-ml) jars

2-inch (5-cm) round cookie cutters

Bubble wrap

Offset spatula

Once set, cut the dough in half. Lightly flour a piece of parchment paper the size of your baking sheet and roll the dough fairly thin, about ⅛ inch (3 mm) thick. Use round cookie cutters that are slightly smaller than the opening of your jars to cut out little rounds. This will ensure the cookie is the correct size for the jar. Remove the excess dough and place the rounds on the parchment-lined baking tray. Poke holes in each round three times with a fork.

Bake for 5 minutes. Do not overbake; they should be semi-soft. Let them cool completely on the pan before transferring them to a cooling rack.

CREAM: In a large bowl, add the cold whipping cream, sour cream, powdered sugar, honey and salt. Beat with an electric mixer until stiff peaks form. Add it to a piping bag and set it in the refrigerator until ready to use.

HONEYCOMB TOPPING: With a marker, trace the diameter of the top of a jar on the back of bubble wrap. Cut out six circles from the bubble wrap and place them on a parchment-lined baking tray. Melt the yellow wafer chocolate with a small amount of brown wafer chocolate to achieve a honey-like color. Spoon the chocolate onto the bubble wrap in a thin layer using the back of a spoon to smooth it out. Once all circles have been covered in chocolate, freeze them on the baking tray until they harden.

ASSEMBLY: Pipe a small amount of cream at the bottom of the jars. Use the 2-inch (5-cm) round cookie cutter to reshape the honey biscuits in a perfect circle. Dunk a honey biscuit into the lavender milk for 3 seconds. Place the biscuit at the bottom of a jelly jar (8 ounces [236 ml]). Pipe a thin layer of cream into the jar. Repeat the layering process until you finish with cream. Each jar should have five honey biscuits with room at the top for the decoration.

Peel the honeycomb chocolate from the bubble wrap and place it on the cake. Trim it with scissors if it doesn't fit perfectly.

☞ *Top with the smallest bit of honey—this step is optional but it adds a great look. It boosts the sweetness, so a little goes a long way.*

Cover the jars with their lids. Refrigerate them overnight. The next day you will have a nice, soft Honey Lavender Jar Cake.

PIPING TECHNIQUES

Piping seems like a daunting skill, but with practice, you can do some amazing things with simple tips. These patterns are basic ones that are all done with various sizes of star tips.

Shell Pattern: Angle the tip so it is slightly above the cake. Squeeze the bag so the icing fans out a bit onto the cake. Release the pressure while lowering the tip toward you onto the cake. Stop squeezing and pull up. Start the next shell right where you left off, slightly overlapping the end of the previous shell.

Star Pattern: Hold the bag parallel to the cake. Giving it a gentle squeeze until the cream touches the cake. Release the pressure and pull up.

Spiral Rope: Pipe a spiral rope by touching the piping tip to the cake at a 45-degree angle. Using your non-dominant hand to guide the bag, with even pressure, gently squeeze and move in a circular motion. The spirals should overlap each other.

Rossette: Hold the tip parallel to the cake. With even pressure, pipe a dollop and continue in a spiral motion as you slightly overlap the cream onto itself to imitate petals. Once you get the desired size, slowly release the pressure and tuck in the tail on the side of the rose.

Peculiar Pies & Tarts

"A PERFECT SLICE OF WHIMSY AND WOE."

fig. 1

fig. 2

fig. 3

FLAKY PIE CRUST

Yield: 1 (9-inch [23-cm]) double crust

Single Batch

3 cups (375 g) all-purpose flour

1 tsp kosher salt

1 tbsp (13 g) granulated sugar

½ cup (96 g) Crisco® vegetable shortening

12 tbsp (170 g) cold unsalted butter, cubed

1 tsp apple cider vinegar

5–7 tbsp (75–105 g) ice-cold water

Double Batch

6 cups (750 g) all-purpose flour

2 tsp (12 g) kosher salt

2 tbsp (25 g) granulated sugar

1 cup (192 g) Crisco vegetable shortening

1½ cups (340 g/3 sticks) cold unsalted butter, cubed

2 tsp (10 g) apple cider vinegar

12–15 tbsp (170–215 g) ice-cold water

In a large mixing bowl, whisk together the flour, salt and sugar until combined. Add the vegetable shortening and cold cubed butter in scattered pieces on top of the flour.

With a pastry cutter, cut in the butter and shortening until the mixture resembles coarse meal (fig. 1). Gently sift the mixture through your fingers to break up any larger chunks. It should have various sized chunks of butter remaining, but the largest pieces should be no bigger than the size of a pea.

Add the vinegar and water and mix it gently with a rubber spatula until the flour has absorbed the water. Do not overmix; the mixture is supposed be shaggy. It will look like many sizes of crumbly chunks that are not formed together into one dough ball (fig. 2).

Dump the dough crumbs onto a clean surface and gather the dough together into a dome. It should look like a brain (fig. 3). Cut it in half and wrap each piece in plastic wrap. Pat it into a disk and chill in the refrigerator for 1 hour.

Roll out and bake according to the temperature and time of your desired recipe. This crust can be prepared ahead and frozen for up to 6 months.

BLUEBERRY GHOST PIES

"GHOSTS AREN'T SEASONAL," A PHRASE TO BE TRUE. AND NEITHER ARE GHOST PIES WITH FILLING SO BLUE. SWEET, TANGY BLUEBERRY, A FACE FULL OF FRIGHT, A PIE CRUST SO FLAKY IT HAUNTS EVERY BITE.

Yield: 18-20 *ghost pies*

Flaky Pie Crust (page 53), double batch

Blueberry Filling

1 lb (454 g) frozen blueberries

½ cup (100 g) granulated sugar

1 tbsp (15 g) lemon juice

½ tsp ground cinnamon

¼ tsp vanilla extract

½ tsp kosher salt

1½ tbsp (15 g) cornstarch

1½ tbsp (23 g) cold water

Special Tools

Ghost template (page 177) or cookie cutter

Round piping tip (Wilton #12)

Pastry brush

Fork

fig. 1

Prepare a double batch of Flaky Pie Crust.

BLUEBERRY FILLING: In a saucepan over medium heat, combine the frozen blueberries, sugar and lemon juice and bring to a simmer, 8 to 10 minutes. Add in the cinnamon, vanilla and salt. Continue to simmer for 1 more minute. In a small cup, mix the cornstarch and cold water to make a slurry. Pour it into the simmering blueberries and immediately stir until thickened. Remove the mixture from the heat and transfer into a bowl to cool completely.

Once the filling is cooled, preheat the oven to 375°F (190°C).

Lightly flour a clean surface and roll the dough out. Fold the dough in half vertically and then horizontally to get four layers. Roll it out one more time to about ¼ inch (6 mm) thick. Using the ghost template as a guide, cut out the shape with a paring knife. Alternatively, a cookie cutter may be used if one is available to you. Remove the excess dough and transfer the cutouts to parchment paper. You may have to use a metal spatula to help scrape them up. Repeat and re-roll the dough until all the dough is used up. Make sure there are two cutouts per pie. If the dough gets soft and overworked, set it in the refrigerator to chill until it becomes workable again.

For the top ghost cutout, use the front of a round piping tip (Wilton #12) to cut out the eyes. Flip the piping tip over to the wide end to cut out the mouth (fig. 1).

(continued)

BLUEBERRY GHOST PIES *continued*

Pasteurized egg whites in a carton,
for brushing

Lemon Glaze

1 cup + 2 tbsp (134 g)
powdered sugar

2 tsp (10 g) lemon juice

2 tbsp (30 g) pasteurized egg
whites in a carton (see Note)

On the bottom of the ghost cutout, add a bit of blueberry filling to the center of the torso and head area. Avoid overfilling or the blueberries will gush out during baking. Dip a finger into water and spread it around the edges of the bottom crust. This will act as glue for the dough to stick together. Add the top crust, press the edges down lightly with your finger, then crimp the edges with a fork. Transfer to a cookie sheet and continue making the rest of the ghosts. Place the ghosts in the freezer for 15 minutes so the crust can firm up.

Brush with pasteurized egg whites and bake for 22 to 24 minutes, or until the filling starts to bubble and the bottoms are golden brown.

LEMON GLAZE: Combine the powdered sugar, lemon juice and pasteurized egg whites together until the mixture is smooth and shiny. Keep the glaze covered while it's not in use because it dries quickly.

Remove the pies from the oven and quickly brush them with the glaze. Let the glaze dry for 10 minutes, then transfer the ghost pies with a spatula to a cooling rack. Repeat for the rest of the ghosts, working one pan at a time. Let them cool before enjoying!

☞ *Carton pasteurized egg whites are safe to consume because they have been heat treated to remove bacteria.*

GRASSHOPPER PIE

SILKY FILLING, A MINTY BREEZE. A PIE SO GREEN IT'S SURE TO ENTICE. HOPPING UPON THIS TREAT OF EASE. A FRIEND WHO'D LIKE TO SHARE A SLICE.

Yield: 1 (9-inch [23-cm]) pie

Cookie Crust

25 Oreo cookies

4 tbsp (60 g) melted butter

½ tsp lime zest

Mint Filling

2 (8-oz [227-g]) blocks cream cheese, softened

1 (14-oz [397-g]) can sweetened condensed milk

½ tsp vanilla extract

1 tsp peppermint extract

2 drops green food dye

2 tsp (6 g) unflavored powdered gelatin

2 tbsp (30 g) cold water

COOKIE CRUST: Obliterate the Oreos into fine crumbs using a food processor or by finely crushing them in a plastic bag with a rolling pin. In a bowl, add the crushed Oreos, melted butter and lime zest. Mix with a fork until it is the texture of wet sand.

Pour the mixture into a 9-inch (23-cm) pie plate. Use the bottom of a flat measuring cup to pack it down on the bottom and up the sides. Place it in the freezer until needed.

MINT FILLING: In a large mixing bowl, beat the cream cheese for 1 minute, until creamy. Add the condensed milk and mix on low for 30 seconds, until combined. Then, add the vanilla, peppermint extract and green food dye. Mix for 30 seconds, until combined.

In a small bowl, mix the cold water and gelatin, then let it sit for 5 minutes. After the gelatin has bloomed, place it in the microwave in 15-second intervals, until it is dissolved. Let it cool before proceeding.

Once the gelatin has cooled, add two heaping spoonfuls of the cream cheese mixture to it and stir until combined. Pour the gelatin mixture into the cream cheese mixture and mix on low speed for 30 seconds. Dump the filling into the chilled cookie crust. Poke any air bubbles with a toothpick and refrigerate for a minimum of 6 hours to firm up.

(continued)

GRASSHOPPER PIE *continued*

Grasshoper Transfer
½ cup (95 g) white wafer chocolate melts

Brown wafer chocolate melts

Oil-based food dye (green, light green, black, brown)

Cream Topping
½ cup (100 g) heavy whipping cream

2 tbsp (25 g) granulated sugar

¼ tsp lime zest

Special Tools
Grasshopper template (page 177)

Clear acetate sheet

Piping bags

Paintbrush

Star piping tip (Wilton #21)

☞ *Though using oil-based food dye to color the white chocolate wafers is preferable for getting exact colors, an alternative would be to purchase the candy wafers already colored.*

GRASSHOPPER TRANSFER: Print out the grasshopper template (page 177) and tape it onto the back of a backing tray. Tape a piece of clear plastic acetate paper over it and set it aside. Alternatively, a thick, clear plastic sandwich bag can be used in place of acetate paper.

Melt the white wafer chocolate in the microwave according to the package directions. Separate the chocolate into four bowls. Color each bowl of chocolate with the oil-based food dyes: green, light green, black and brown. Oil-based food dye must be used to color chocolate—all other food dyes will cause the chocolate to seize. To darken some colors, melting the smallest piece of brown chocolate wafer melts works great.

Fill the piping bags with chocolate one color at a time since the chocolate sets quickly. If all the bags are filled at once, the chocolate that is sitting will harden in the bag and will be difficult to remelt.

Starting with the black chocolate, fill a piping bag and cut the tip as small as the lines on the template. Trace the black outlines of the grasshopper over the acetate paper. Use a toothpick dipped in chocolate to draw any thin lines that the piping bag can't get. Once all the black has been drawn, let it sit for 10 minutes, until the chocolate has hardened.

Continue to add the other colors, making sure to let the chocolate harden between each color. Use a paintbrush for the brown and light green parts of the grasshopper to soften any hard lines and give it blending effect. Leave the darker green for last, as this is the base color. Pipe it over the whole image and cover the black outline to create a green border. The whole black part should be covered in dark green to make the design sturdy. Allow the grasshopper to harden. Meanwhile, make the cream topping.

CREAM TOPPING: In a medium bowl, add the heavy cream, sugar and lime zest. Beat until stiff peaks form. Fit a piping bag with a small star tip (Wilton #21).

ASSEMBLY: Flip the chocolate grasshopper in the center of the pie. Gently peel back the clear acetate sheet. Pipe cream around the pie in a shell pattern (page 49). Pipe little star dollops around the grasshopper.

This pie is best eaten cold. Store covered in the refrigerator for 3 to 5 days.

SCARY CHERRY PIE

WITH CRIMSON FILLING THE CHERRY FACE CRIES, DOOMED BY ITS DEVOURING FATE. IT'S TRULY THE CREEPIEST OF CHERRY PIES, WITH A FACE THAT ONLY ITS MOTHER WON'T HATE.

Yield: 1 (9-inch [23-cm]) pie

Flaky Pie Crust (page 53), single batch

3 tbsp (22 g) panko breadcrumbs, divided

Cherry Filling

2 lb (907 g) frozen sweet dark cherries, pitted

⅓ cup + 1 tbsp (80 g) granulated sugar

¼ tsp lemon zest

2 tbsp (30 g) lemon juice

½ tsp kosher salt

½ tsp ground ginger

¾ tsp almond extract

¼ tsp vanilla extract

2 tbsp (28 g) unsalted butter

⅓ cup (80 g) maraschino cherry syrup (from the jar of cherries)

¼ cup (35 g) cornstarch

Milk, for brushing

Slivered almonds, for teeth

Vanilla ice cream, for serving (optional)

☞ *It is best to use an aluminum pie tin for this recipe: 1. for aesthetics and 2. because they conduct heat better than ceramic or glass pans. This will result in a crisp and sturdy base for the pie.*

Prepare a single batch of the Flaky Pie Crust. Let it chill for an hour to firm up. The most important part while working with this crust is keeping it cool or else it will become difficult to handle. Patience is key.

CHERRY FILLING: In a large pot over medium heat, combine the frozen cherries, sugar, lemon zest, lemon juice, salt, ginger, almond extract and vanilla. Bring to a simmer for 7 to 10 minutes, until the cherries are thawed and their juices come to a rolling simmer. Add in the butter and stir until melted, then bring it back to a simmer. In a small bowl, combine the maraschino cherry syrup and cornstarch to create a slurry. Add it to the simmering pot and stir constantly until the mixture becomes as thick as jam. Remove it from the heat and pour the filling onto a parchment-lined baking sheet. Spread it in a single layer to cool completely. Meanwhile, prepare the crust.

Working with one pie disk, lightly flour a piece of parchment paper and a rolling pin. Roll the dough out to ⅛-inch (3-mm) thickness. Fold the dough onto itself in half vertically and then horizontally to get four layers. Roll it out one more time into a rough circle. Sprinkle 1½ tablespoons (11 g) of bread-crumbs at the bottom of a 9-inch (23-cm) pie tin. Transfer the dough by turning it over with the parchment paper into the pie tin. Peel off the parchment paper and fold the excess dough under itself to make the rim of the crust. Crimp the edges, if desired, and place the pie tin in the freezer for 20 minutes, or until it is solid. Freezing the pie crust will prevent it from getting soggy during baking.

(continued)

fig. 1

fig. 2

fig. 3

fig. 4

SCARY CHERRY PIE *continued*

THE FACE: A few things before we begin. Just like people, each face will look different. Pie dough is a finicky material that shouldn't be overworked. Just let the dough do what it will. The goal is to get a scary face, so trying to make it look pretty is pointless. This pie crust is easier to work with when it's cold. If it gets too soft or springy, wrap it up and allow it to relax in the freezer for 15 minutes. With that said . . .

Using the second pie disk, lightly flour a piece of parchment paper and roll the dough out. Fold the dough in half vertically and then horizontally to get four layers. Roll it out one more time into a rough circle. Roughly measure a circle 1 inch (2.5 cm) larger than the diameter of the pie tin. Cut out the eyes and mouth with a paring knife. Slide the face with the parchment paper onto a baking tray and refrigerate until needed.

To create the features on the face, cooked pieces of pie dough will be placed under the main face to create dimension on the nose, cheeks and brow bone.

Estimate where you'd like the dimension of the face to be and sculpt them out of the excess dough on a parchment-lined baking sheet (fig. 1). Remember to make them a bit thinner than you would expect because they will expand a bit during baking. Freeze for 15 minutes, then bake at 425°F (220°C) for 10 to 12 minutes, until golden brown. Let them cool.

Carefully place the baked pieces under the uncooked pie face and gently sculpt them into place. Freeze the face for 15 more minutes to firm up (fig. 2).

Meanwhile, sprinkle the last 1½ tablespoons (11 g) of breadcrumbs on the bottom of the frozen pie tin crust. Add in the cooled cherry filling and spread it flat.

Once the face has chilled, gently peel it off the parchment paper and place it on top of the cherry filling. Trim any overhang so that the face fits perfectly within the walls of the bottom crust (fig. 3). Don't crimp the edges of the face to the bottom crust. The gap between will allow the filling to bubble over and enhance the gore factor. The more deformed and cherry splattered, the better.

Poke nostril holes with a skewer or toothpick and chill the whole pie in the freezer for 15 more minutes, or until it is solid.

Brush the top with milk and place the pie on the lowest rack of the oven. Bake at 425°F (220°C) for 20 minutes, then reduce the heat to 375°F (190°C) and bake for an additional 1 hour and 10 minutes. Move the pie to the top rack during the last 10 minutes. It is done when the crust is golden brown and the filling starts to bubble. If the face is browning too quickly, lightly tent it with foil halfway through baking.

Remove the pie from the oven and allow it to cool for about 4 hours before cutting into it. This will give the filling time to firm up. Add slivered almonds in the mouth to imitate teeth. Serve with a scoop of vanilla ice cream, if desired. Oh, and don't be scared. It's just cherry pie.

Store the pie covered at room temperature for up to 2 days.

STRAWBERRY LADYBUG PIES

FLAKY RED BEETLES, A SWEET INFESTATION. STUFFED WITH STRAWBERRIES AND ALMOND GALORE. PAINTED WITH ICING, THIS PERFECT CREATION IS SURELY A PASTRY ONE CANNOT IGNORE.

Yield: 10 pies

Pink Crust
Flaky Pie Crust (page 53), double batch

6 drops red gel food dye

Strawberry Filling
1 lb (454 g) fresh strawberries

⅓ cup (67 g) granulated sugar

1 tbsp (15 g) lemon juice

1 tsp lemon zest

1 tbsp (21 g) honey

¼ tsp kosher salt

1½ tsp (7 g) vanilla extract

1 tsp strawberry extract

2 tbsp (10 g) cornstarch

2 tbsp (30 g) cold water

Almond Frangipane
6 tbsp (84 g) butter, softened

⅓ cup (67 g) granulated sugar

1 large egg

¼ tsp almond extract

1 cup (110 g) almond flour

½ tbsp (5 g) cornstarch

PINK CRUST: Prepare the double batch of Flaky Pie Crust. Add the red food dye to the 12 to 15 tablespoons (170 to 215 g) of ice-cold water before adding it into the crust mixture. Proceed with the recipe as written. The final crust will have specks of white butter. This will go away when baked.

STRAWBERRY FILLING: Cut the strawberries into ½-inch (1.3-cm) pieces, making sure to remove and discard the stems. Add them to a medium saucepan along with the sugar, lemon juice, lemon zest, honey, salt, vanilla and strawberry extract. Heat on medium-low temp and bring the mixture to a gentle simmer for 1 minute. Just as the mixture begins to simmer, mix the cornstarch and cold water in a small cup to make a slurry. Dump it into the strawberries and mix for 30 seconds until thickened. Remove the pan from the heat and empty them on a plate. Spread them in a thin layer to cool completely before using.

☞ *Avoid cooking the strawberries for too long. They turn into mush within seconds. You still want the strawberries to be chunky.*

ALMOND FRANGIPANE: With an electric mixer, cream the butter and sugar for 2 minutes, until fluffy. Add the egg and almond extract and beat for 2 more minutes. Finally, add the almond flour and cornstarch and mix until combined. Add the frangipane to a piping bag.

ASSEMBLY: Line a baking tray with parchment paper and set aside. Roll out the pie dough on a piece of parchment paper ¼ inch (6 mm) thick. Fold the dough onto itself in half vertically and then horizontally to get four layers. Roll it out one more time into a rough circle. Using the template and a paring knife, cut out the shape. Each pie will have two cutouts. Place all the bottom cutouts on a parchment-lined baking sheet. They will be assembled on the tray.

(continued)

Red Icing

1 cup + 2 tbsp (134 g) powdered sugar

1 tsp lemon juice

2 tbsp (30 g) pasteurized carton egg whites

Red gel food dye

Black Icing

1 cup (120 g) powdered sugar

1½ tbsp (23 g) pasteurized egg whites from a carton

½ tsp lemon juice

Black gel food dye

Special Tools

Ladybug template (page 177)

Piping bags

Round piping tip (Wilton #2)

Paintbrush

Pipe a thin layer of frangipane on the head and abdomen, then spoon a bit of strawberry filling in the center making sure not to overstuff it. Run a wet finger around the perimeter of the crust, then add the top crust. Crimp all the way around by gently pressing down on the edges. Crimp again with a fork all the way around. With a fork, prick vertical vent holes down the center of the back of the pie where the wings separate. Once all the pies have been assembled, place them in the freezer for 20 minutes.

Meanwhile, preheat the oven to 375°F (190°C) and prepare the icing glaze.

ICING: Whisk together the powdered sugar, lemon juice and pasteurized egg whites until thin and glossy. Add the red food dye and mix. Avoid adding too much food dye or it could potentially alter the taste of the icing. Cover the bowl with plastic wrap to prevent it from drying.

Prepare the black icing in a separate bowl by whisking together the powdered sugar, pasteurized egg whites and lemon juice. It will be thicker than the red icing. Set aside 2 tablespoons (32 g) of white icing before dying the whole bowl with the black food dye. Cover with plastic wrap and set aside until needed.

Bake the pies for 25 to 28 minutes, until the bottoms are slightly browned. Let them cool for 7 minutes before transferring the pies to a cooling rack.

Once they are cool to the touch, dunk the tops of the pies facedown into the red icing and let the excess drip off. Use a pastry brush to help get the sides for a smooth finish. Set them on a cooling rack to dry.

👉 *To get the smoothest finish, avoid touching the pie after it has been dunked. Working quickly is key. Naturally some pie crust flakes may get into the icing. Be gentle with the pie to prevent this from happening too much. Let them dry before adding the black icing.*

Add the black icing to a piping bag with a round piping tip (Wilton #2). Working one ladybug at a time, pipe on the head. Use a paintbrush to spread the icing around the top and the sides. Pipe a line of black down the middle of the back to create the wings. Pipe black dots on the wings. Lastly, pipe small white details to the head and back. Let them dry and enjoy! Store in the refrigerator for up to 2 days.

APPLE EYE PIES

SPICED APPLE FILLING GUSHES THROUGHOUT, WHILE GLOSSY EYEBALLS PEER ALL ABOUT. ODDEST OF PEARS, APPLE AND EYE. A BEWITCHING ALLURE ONE CANNOT DENY.

Yield: 15 pies

Flaky Pie Crust (page 53), single batch

Eyeballs

2 very firm Bosc pears, skin on (see Note)

White soft gel paste food dye (AmeriColor®)

3 drops vodka

White chocolate candy wafer melts

Oil-based food dye (blue, black, white)

Piping gel

Apple Filling

2 tbsp (28 g) unsalted butter

3 cups (365 g) diced firm apples (Granny Smith, Fuji, Golden Delicious)

6 tbsp (83 g) dark brown sugar

¼ tsp cinnamon

⅛ tsp cardamom

⅛ tsp nutmeg

⅛ tsp ground ginger

¼ tsp salt

⅓ cup (83 g) cherry juice

½ tbsp (8 g) lemon juice

½ tsp vanilla extract

½ tbsp (5 g) cornstarch

½ tbsp (8 g) cold water

2 drops red food dye

Prepare a single batch of Flaky Pie Crust.

EYEBALLS: With a melon baller about 1-teaspoon large, gouge out half spheres from the pears, skin on.

☞ It is important that the pears be quite firm to minimize the amount of shrinkage during baking.

Try to get as many spheres as possible. Dice the remainder of the pear carcasses and set aside for the apple filling. Place the half spheres on a piece of parchment paper and pat them dry with a paper towel.

To make the white paint, add a quarter-sized amount of the white soft gel paste to a small bowl along with 3 small drops of vodka. Mix it together until it is a paintable consistency. Paint the pear spheres and set them aside to dry.

☞ Even though vodka is used to make edible paint, it is still safe for kids. The small amount of alcohol acts as a drying agent and evaporates while the paint dries.

APPLE FILLING: Brown the butter by adding it to a small pan over medium heat. Gently swirl the pan so the butter melts evenly. When the butter starts to bubble, stir with a rubber spatula. As soon as it turns a caramel brown color and the aroma smells of toasted nuts, it is done. Immediately transfer the browned butter into a bowl, including the brown little bits (they hold all the flavor), and set it aside.

Peel, core and dice the apples. Place them in a large saucepan along with the reserved pear leftovers, brown sugar, cinnamon, cardamom, nutmeg, ground ginger and salt. Stir until the sugar is dissolved and the apples start leaching their juices, 3 to 5 minutes. Add the cherry juice, lemon juice and vanilla and simmer for about 3 minutes, until the apples are tender but not too soft.

(continued)

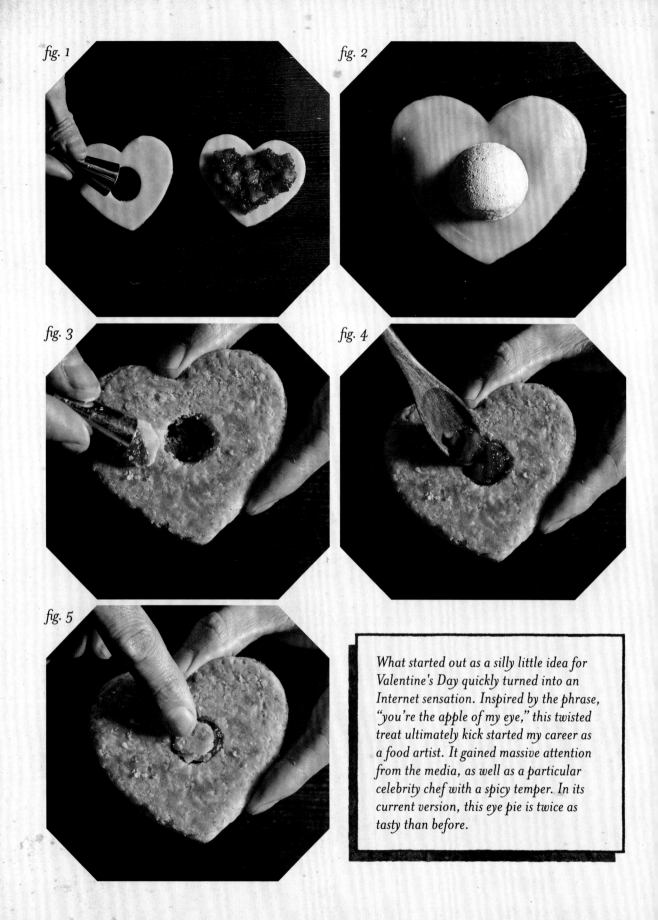

fig. 1

fig. 2

fig. 3

fig. 4

fig. 5

What started out as a silly little idea for Valentine's Day quickly turned into an Internet sensation. Inspired by the phrase, "you're the apple of my eye," this twisted treat ultimately kick started my career as a food artist. It gained massive attention from the media, as well as a particular celebrity chef with a spicy temper. In its current version, this eye pie is twice as tasty than before.

Egg Wash
1 egg white

1 tsp water

Turbinado sugar

Special Tools
Melon baller

3½-inch (9-cm) heart cookie cutter

1½-inch (4-cm) circle cookie cutter

Small and large piping tip

Piping bags

Paintbrushes

In a small cup, combine the cornstarch and cold water to create a slurry. Dump it into the swimming apples and stir immediately until the mixture thickens. Remove from the heat and dump the filling into a bowl. Add the brown butter and red food dye, mix and let it cool completely before assembling.

ASSEMBLY: Roll out the dough and cut out shapes using a heart cookie cutter. Each pie requires two hearts. Set them on a piece of parchment paper. Re-roll the excess dough and cut out 1½-inch (4-cm) circles. Cut the circles in half to create the eyelids.

Lay out the bottom heart shapes on a parchment-lined baking tray. Fill the bottom hearts with pie filling. Don't overstuff them or they will burst open while baking. Dip your finger in water and trace a very small amount along the outside of the dough.

For the top dough heart, use the large end of a large piping tip that is about the diameter of the pear spere. Use it to cut a hole in the center (fig. 1). Place the top dough heart on top of the pie filling and add a pear sphere to the center (fig. 2). Press down the edges to close the dough and crimp it closed with a fork. To add the eyelids, run a wet finger on the dough around the pear sphere; this will help the eyelids stick. Place the eyelids on the top and bottom to create an eye shape. Blend them in well by gently pressing the edges into the crust. It is okay if the dough looks a bit wonky; it adds to the horror. There should be filling left over. Set it aside for later.

Freeze the pies for 20 to 30 minutes so that the crust can firm up. Meanwhile, preheat the oven to 425°F (220°C) and line a baking tray with parchment paper.

EGG WASH: Lightly whisk the egg white with the water. Once the pies have firmed up, transfer them to the room-temperature lined baking tray. Brush the crusts with the egg wash. Avoid getting egg wash on the eyeball area and on the parchment paper around the pies. This will cause the egg to burn. Sprinkle turbinado sugar on the crust only to avoid discoloration of the eyeball.

(continued)

APPLE EYE PIES *continued*

Bake the pies for 10 minutes, rotate the pan, then lower the oven temperature to 375°F (190°C) and bake for an additional 15 to 17 minutes. Once the pies have baked, allow them to cool on the pan. The eyes will pull away from the lids a bit during cooling.

Use the larger end of a small piping tip to remove a tiny circle of crust from the back center of the pie (fig. 3). Fill the hole with a few small chunks of apple filling until the eye is pressed up against the lids (fig. 4). Close the hole with the tiny circle of crust (fig. 5).

DECORATION: Melt a large handful of the white wafer chocolate melts as directed on the package. Separate the chocolate into three small bowls. Dye them with oil-based food dye in the colors grayish blue, black and light blue. These shades can all be achieved by mixing blue, black and white in different ways.

☛ *Oil-based food dye must be used for this. Water-based food dye will cause the chocolate to seize. These chocolate melts are sold already dyed if you'd like to forgo using oil-based food dye.*

Working one color at a time, add the grayish blue to a piping bag and set the other colors aside. I like to store the chocolate that is not in use in a microwave that has been heated up for a minute to keep the chocolate from hardening.

Snip a small hole in the piping bag and pipe a circle in the middle of the eye to create the iris. Use a toothpick to correct any imperfections. Repeat for all the pies. Using the black chocolate, snip a tiny hole in the piping bag and pipe a border around the iris and a pupil in the center of the eye. Repeat for all the pies. Lastly, use a small paintbrush to stipple a small amount of light blue chocolate on the iris and around the pupil. Let it dry. If there is any filling left over, brush it on the corner of the eyeballs to make them look bloodshot. Pipe and brush the eyeball with piping gel to give it a realistic glaze.

These eerie delights are good alone or with a bowl of vanilla ice cream. Store any leftovers in an airtight container in the refrigerator for up to 2 days.

BUTTERSCOTCH TARTAN TART

LAID UPON A SHORTBREAD CRUST, THREADS OF ICING, A FANCIFUL SIGHT. THIS TEATIME TREAT IS TRULY A MUST. WITH BUTTERSCOTCH WOVEN THOUGH EVERY BITE.

Yield: 1 (9-inch [23-cm]) tart

Shortbread Tart Shell

1½ cups (188 g) all-purpose flour

1½ tbsp (15 g) cornstarch

3 tbsp (39 g) granulated sugar

¼ tsp kosher salt

½ cup (113 g/1 stick) unsalted butter, melted

Butterscotch Filling

½ cup (113 g/1 stick) cold unsalted butter

½ cup (100 g) dark brown sugar, lightly packed

1 (14-oz [397-g]) can sweetened condensed milk

½ tsp kosher salt

1 tsp vanilla extract

Preheat the oven to 350°F (180°C).

SHORTBREAD TART SHELL: In a medium mixing bowl, whisk together the flour, cornstarch, sugar and salt. Make a well in the center and pour in the melted butter. Stir with a fork until the flour has absorbed the butter and there are large, moist crumbles throughout. Dump two-thirds of the crumbly dough into a 9-inch (23-cm) tart pan and firmly press it along the sides. Dump the rest in and press it into the bottom. Use a flat measuring cup to help pack in the crust. Freeze it for 15 minutes.

Prick the bottom of the shell with a fork. This tart shell is blind baked, which means it's baked without a filling. Crumple up some parchment paper, open it up again and place it on top of the tart shell. Add enough dry beans or pie weights to fill all the way to the top of the pan. Trim the excess parchment paper and bake for 25 minutes, then remove the parchment and weights by carefully lifting the parchment with both hands.

Continue to bake the tart for 7 to 10 more minutes, until the edges are golden brown. If the parchment sticks to the bottom of the crust, it just means that it needs to bake a bit longer. Set the tart shell on a cooling rack to cool completely before proceeding.

BUTTERSCOTCH FILLING: In a small nonstick pot on low heat, add the cold butter, brown sugar, condensed milk and salt. Whisk constantly until the mixture reaches 240°F (115°C), about 15 minutes. Do not increase the heat—low and slow is key. As the mixture thickens, it will have to be whisked a bit faster because it will begin to split closer to the target temperature. It will look wrong, but it is correct. Just keep mixing.

(continued)

BUTTERSCOTCH TARTAN TART *continued*

Royal Icing

1¾ cups (210 g) powdered sugar, plus more if needed

1 tsp lemon juice, plus more if needed

2½ tbsp (38 g) pasteurized carton egg whites or whole milk

Gel food dye (red, black)

Special Tools

9-inch (23-cm) tart pan

Dry beans or pie weights

Round piping tip (Wilton #2)

Piping bags

Tartan template (page 177)

Sewing pin

Once the butterscotch reaches its target temperature, remove the pot from the heat and quickly stir in the vanilla. Whisk until the excess oil is incorporated and the butterscotch is thick and runny. Pour the butterscotch into the cooled tart shell and shake the pan on a flat surface to even it out. Refrigerate it for 1 hour to firm up.

ROYAL ICING: Mix the powdered sugar, lemon juice and pasteurized egg whites in a bowl until thick and glossy. The consistency should be of thick glue. It should be thick enough to hold its shape when piped. If the icing is too thin, add 1 tablespoon (8 g) more of powdered sugar. If it is too thin, add ½ teaspoon more of lemon juice.

Divide the icing up, with red being the least amount needed. Color one portion red, another black and leave the rest white. Use a round piping tip (Wilton #2) to pipe all the lines.

To transfer the plaid pattern, cut out the tartan template along with a piece of parchment paper the same size in diameter. Lay the parchment paper on the firm butterscotch tart and lay the template on top. With a sewing pin, poke little holes along the lines to transfer the image. This is a similar technique for transferring a design onto a pumpkin. To differentiate the lines, poke holes farther apart for the long running lines and closer together for the black stitch lines. Once all the lines have been poked remove the pattern and parchment paper and begin piping.

With the royal icing in piping bags, pipe the red lines first. Let them dry for 15 minutes, then pipe the white lines. Let those dry for 15 to 20 minutes, then add the black and let it dry. Remove the tart from the pan and enjoy! This tart is best served at room temperature when it is gooey.

Store covered in the refrigerator for up to a week.

PUMPKIN ROSE CHIFFON PIE

Essence of rose, a subtle perfume, mingles with pumpkin, creating a bloom. Light fluffy filling on graham cracker crust, this pie is surely a holiday must. An unusual pair, pumpkin and rose. A pie that appeases your stomach and nose.

Yield: 1 (9-inch [23-cm]) pie

Graham Cracker Crust

1½ cups (188 g) graham cracker crumbs

3 tbsp (39 g) granulated sugar

6 tbsp (85 g) unsalted butter, melted

Pumpkin Chiffon Filling

¼ cup (50 g) cold water

1 (8-g) envelope unflavored powdered gelatin

3 large eggs, separated

½ cup (100 g) granulated sugar, divided

¼ cup (50 g) whole milk

¼ cup (60 g) full-fat sour cream

½ tsp salt

½ tsp nutmeg

½ tsp ginger

½ tsp cinnamon

1 cup (250 g) canned pumpkin puree

1 tsp vanilla extract

Preheat the oven to 375°F (190°C).

GRAHAM CRACKER CRUST: Obliterate the graham crackers into fine crumbs using a food processor or by crushing them in a plastic bag with a rolling pin. In a bowl, add the crushed graham crackers, sugar and melted butter and mix until the mixture resembles wet sand.

Dump the crumbs out into a 9-inch (23-cm) pie plate. Use a flat-bottomed measuring cup to help firmly pack the crumbs into the bottom and up the sides of the pie plate. Bake the crust for 7 to 10 minutes and let cool.

PUMPKIN CHIFFON FILLING: Create a double boiler by adding 1 inch (2.5 cm) of water to a small sauce pot. Bring it to a simmer on low heat. In a small cup, mix the cold water and unflavored gelatin and set it aside to bloom.

Add the egg yolks to a heatproof mixing bowl along with ¼ cup (50 g) of sugar, milk, sour cream, salt, nutmeg, ginger and cinnamon. Whisk until incorporated. Rest the bowl over the pot of simmering water, making sure that the water doesn't touch the bottom of the bowl. Whisk constantly until the mixture reaches 140°F (62°C). Add in the bloomed gelatin puck and stir until the gelatin is completely dissolved and the temperature reaches 155°F (68°C). Remove the bowl from the heat and stir in the pumpkin puree and vanilla with a rubber spatula until combined. Set the mixture aside to cool.

(continued)

Rose Topping

½ cup (100 g) heavy whipping cream

2 tbsp (25 g) granulated sugar

¼ tsp rose water (see Note)

1 drop pink food dye

Toasted, unsalted pumpkin seeds, for garnish

Special Tools

9-inch (23-cm) pie plate

Piping bag

Star piping tip (Wilton #2D)

Keep an electric hand mixer handy. In a separate heatproof bowl, add the egg whites and the remaining ¼ cup (50 g) of sugar and whisk until incorporated. Place the bowl over the double boiler and whisk constantly until the temperature reaches 155°F (68°C). Immediately remove from the heat and beat with the hand mixer until the mixture comes to room temperature and forms stiff peaks, 8 to 10 minutes.

Add ½ cup (106 g) of the cooled egg yolk and pumpkin mixture to the egg whites and gently fold it in to loosen the batter. Now add all the egg white mixture to the egg yolk and pumpkin mixture and gently fold it in with a rubber spatula until no streaks remain. Pour the mixture into the cooled pie crust, level it out with an offset spatula and refrigerate for 6 hours or overnight for the best results.

ROSE TOPPING: Once the pie has set, beat the heavy whipping cream, sugar, rose water and pink food dye with an electric mixer until stiff peaks form. Put the cream in a piping bag affixed with a closed star piping tip (Wilton #2D). Hold the piping bag straight up so that the piping tip is parallel with the pie. Starting at the center of the pie and working your way out, pipe in a slightly overlapping spiral to create a giant rosette (page 49). Garnish the exposed parts of the pie with pumpkin seeds.

This pie is best enjoyed cold. It will keep for 3 to 5 days in the refrigerator.

For the cream topping, if you aren't a fan of rose, swap the rose water out for ½ teaspoon of pumpkin pie spice for a traditional variation.

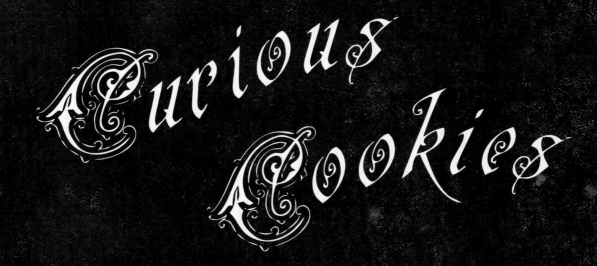

Curious Cookies

"WITH FLAVORS QUITE ODD AND SHAPES SO RARE, EACH
COOKIE WILL HOLD A WONDEROUS FLAIR."

HERB GARDEN SHORTBREAD

ROSEMARY WHISPERS WITH A LEMONY BREEZE. THYME FOR PROSPERITY AND SAGE TO APPEASE. A BUTTERY BISCUIT WITH A TEXTURE SO FINE. A MAGICAL JOURNEY THAT'S OH SO DIVINE.

Yield: 1 (9-inch [23-cm]) *pie dish*

....

1¾ cups (219 g) all-purpose flour

2 tbsp (20 g) cornstarch

½ tsp kosher salt

1 tbsp (4 g) fresh rosemary

1 cup (226 g/2 sticks) unsalted butter, softened

½ cup (100 g) granulated sugar

1 tsp lemon zest (about 1 large lemon)

1 tsp lemon juice

1 egg white

1 tsp water

Turbinado sugar, for sprinkling

Fresh herbs (rosemary, thyme, sage, parsley)

To line a 9-inch (23-cm) pie dish with parchment paper, crumple the parchment paper, open it up and lay it flat on the bottom of the pie dish.

In a medium bowl, whisk together the flour, cornstarch, salt and rosemary. Set it aside. In a large bowl, beat the butter, sugar, lemon zest and lemon juice with an electric mixer for 3 minutes, until light and fluffy. Add the dry ingredients and beat on low speed until the mixture becomes shaggy crumbles. Don't overmix. Fold in using a rubber spatula until no flour remains and the dough just comes together.

Dump the dough into the pie dish and moderately press with lightly floured hands until the top is smooth. Try not to press too hard. With a knife, deeply score the shortbread into diamond shapes or any shapes you desire. Trim away the overhang parchment paper and refrigerate for 1 hour to firm. Once chilled, preheat the oven to 375°F (190°C).

To make the egg wash, lightly whisk together the egg white and water. Evenly brush the top of the shortbread with the egg wash. Prick the center of each dough diamond with a fork, then press a singular herb leaf in the center of each diamond. Sprinkle with turbinado sugar and bake for 30 to 35 minutes, until golden brown. Let it sit for 1 hour to cool before re-scoring the lines all the way down to the bottom of the pan.

Now for one of the most important steps. Drying the shortbread will give it a delicate texture that melts in your mouth. Heat the oven back up to 375°F (190°C) for 10 minutes. Take the shortbread out of the pie dish and space them out on a parchment-lined baking sheet. Turn the oven off, then place the shortbread cookies back in. The decreasing heat will dry them out. After 1 hour, remove them from the oven and let them cool to room temperature.

Store any leftovers in an airtight container for up to 3 weeks. They taste better with age.

GINGERSNAP LANTERN

Yield: 1 *lantern*

....

WITHIN GLOWING WINDOWS, A MARVEL ENSHRINED. A BEAUTIFUL STAR THAT IS SWEETLY CONFINED. THE GINGERSNAP LANTERN GLEAMS WITH A FLARE, AS WARM WINTER SPICES WAFT THROUGH THE AIR.

Gingersnap Dough

1½ cups (188 g) ground graham crackers (about 12 graham crackers)

3 cups (375 g) all-purpose flour

1¼ tsp (6 g) baking soda

3 tsp (8 g) ground cinnamon

2 tsp (4 g) ground ginger

¾ tsp freshly grated nutmeg

Heaping ¼ tsp ground cloves

Heaping ¼ tsp kosher salt

¾ cup (170 g/1½ sticks) butter, softened

1½ cups (330 g) dark brown sugar

2 large eggs

½ tsp vanilla extract

Print and cut out the lantern templates on page 177.

GINGERSNAP DOUGH: Add the ground graham crackers to a medium bowl along with the flour, baking soda, cinnamon, ginger, nutmeg, cloves and salt. Whisk it together and set it aside. In a large bowl, beat the butter and brown sugar. Add the eggs and beat until combined. On low speed, mix in the dry ingredients a little at a time until incorporated—don't overmix.

Gather the dough into a ball. Place the dough on a 26-inch (65-cm)-long sheet of parchment paper and pat it down into a square. On a second 26-inch (65-cm) sheet of parchment paper, draw a 12 x 24–inch (30 x 60–cm) rectangle with a non-toxic marker. Place it ink side up on top of the dough, then roll the dough out within the boundary of the marked rectangle. Any dough that goes over the markings can be cut off and added back inside the marked rectangle. The slab should have an even thickness of about ⅛ inch (3 mm) and the overhang should be minimal.

☞ *Roll from the center of the dough outwards to the mark-ings. This will ensure the cookie will bake evenly. Check both sides of the sheet of dough to make sure they are smooth in case the parchment paper is crinkled on the bottom.*

With scissors, cut through the paper and dough on the marked lines. Cut the slab down the middle to get two 12 x 12–inch (30 x 30–cm) sheets of dough. Slide them on top of each other on a baking tray and freeze for 30 minutes. Wrap and refrigerate any excess dough in case of any mishaps. Preheat the oven to 350°F (180°C) and line a baking tray with parchment paper.

(continued)

Sugar Windows

1 cup (200 g) granulated sugar

⅓ cup (113 g) corn syrup

2 tbsp (30 g) water

1 tsp vanilla extract

Cornstarch, for dusting

Royal Icing

1¾ cups (210 g) powdered sugar

1 tsp lemon juice

2 tbsp (30 g) pasteurized egg whites in a carton

Gel food dye (black, brown, orange, yellow)

Special Tools

Gingersnap Lantern template (page 177)

Exacto knife

Instant-read thermometer

Microplane (citrus zester)

Piping bags

Piping tip (Wilton #2)

3 food cans (not empty)

Small battery-operated LED light

Once the dough is chilled, remove the parchment paper and place it on the lined baking tray. Depending on the size of your baking trays, you may have to bake the dough slabs separately. If that is the case, leave one slab in the freezer until it is ready to bake.

These are twice baked. Bake the first time for 13 minutes, until partially baked. Let the cookie sit in the pan for 10 minutes before sliding it onto a cutting board. Let the slabs cool completely before proceeding.

CUTTING THE SHAPES: Arrange the lantern templates on the cookie slabs in a strategic way to minimize the number of extra irregularly shaped cookies being used. This will leave you with extra material in case of errors.

With a sharp knife, carefully cut out the shapes. Be sure to leave the cut-outs on the parchment so they don't deform. With an exacto knife, cut out the star shapes on the steeple pieces and use a toothpick and skewer to poke extra dots to look like small stars. Remove the excess cookie and set aside in case of any mess ups or as a snack for later.

Once all the pieces have been cut, slide the parchment paper with the pieces on it onto a baking tray and bake a second time for 8 to 10 minutes, until the cookies are a bit darker. Leave them to cool and crisp up.

SUGAR WINDOWS: Lightly butter and crumble up a large piece of parchment paper. It should be big enough to fit all the window pieces. Open the parchment back up and place it on a baking tray. This will help create a texture in the windows. Lay the window template pieces down on the parchment as flat as possible and set them aside.

To a small sauce pot, add the sugar, corn syrup, water and vanilla. Mix it up until combined, then turn the burner to medium heat. Cover the pot and let the sugar simmer undisturbed for 5 minutes. Do not stir the mixture at any point or the sugar will crystallize. After 5 minutes, remove the lid and let the mixture simmer until it starts to turn amber in color and the temperature reaches 345 to 350°F (180°C) when tested with an instant-read thermometer. Take the mixture off the burner and immediately pour it into a heatproof measuring cup with a spout. Let it sit until most of the bubbles dissipate at about 265°F (129°C). Have a cup of water on hand. It's a good place to put the sticky thermometer for an easier cleanup.

Carefully pour the hot sugar mixture into the center of the windowpanes in a steady stream. Work with haste or the sugar will harden. Allow the windows to cool. Once hardened, dust both sides with a light dusting of cornstarch. This will keep the windows from melting and getting sticky.

Meanwhile, prepare the other pieces by taking a microplane (citrus zester) and angling the sides of the cookies at about 45-degree angles so when they connect, they create a corner. It's okay if there are gaps because they will be covered up with icing later. Save the cookie dust that falls from the microplane.

☞ *Note that the cookies will break if too much pressure is applied. In most cases, broken cookies can be repaired with royal icing.*

Angle the windowpanes once the sugar inside has hardened.

ROYAL ICING: Whisk together the powdered sugar, lemon juice and pasteurized egg whites in a medium bowl until thick. Set a small amount aside and color it black. Add it to a piping bag. Color the rest of the icing close to the color of the cookies. A mixture of brown and small amounts of black, orange and yellow will make a color close to the cookie. It doesn't have to be exact. Add it to a piping bag, with a (Wilton #2) tip attached.

ASSEMBLY: Place a windowpane piece on the template. With the black royal icing, follow the diagonal lines across the windows to create a leaded lattice pattern. Let it dry. Once dry, build the lantern in sections by gluing the pieces with brown royal icing. Start with the top pieces so they have adequate time to dry before stacking. Pipe the icing into the corner cracks to close the gaps. Smooth it out in a line with a finger and gently press in the cookie dust from earlier. It's okay if it looks dusty now. It will be brushed when it dries. This step will help the corners look seamless. Use food cans to help keep the windowpane sections up while drying.

Once all the elements are built and dried, glue the roof to the window panels with royal icing and cover up any gaps with icing and cookie dust. Once dry, place a small LED light on the base and add the lantern on top. Watch how the lantern illuminates in the darkness. The lantern doesn't have to be glued to the base for easy access to the light. This lantern makes the perfect edible centerpiece.

Bake any excess cookies off into the shape of stars to display with the lantern. Do not let the scraps go to waste. Any extra pieces taste great with tea or coffee.

PUMPKIN WHOOPIE PIES

VELVETY PUMPKINS WITH SPICES ENTWINED. ARE MARVELS OF CAKE AND COOKIE COMBINED. THEIR CREAMY SAGE CENTERS DO MAKE THEM REFINED. WITH SPIRIT OF AUTUMN, THESE TREATS ARE ALIGNED.

Yield: 15 *whoopie pies*

Modeling Chocolate Stems

1 (12-oz [350-g]) bag white melting chocolate candy wafers

¼ cup (84 g) light corn syrup

Gel food dye (brown, green, yellow)

Sage Cream Filling

1 cup (226 g/2 sticks) unsalted butter, softened

1 tbsp (2 g) fresh sage, chopped

¾ cup (150 g) granulated sugar

3 tbsp (30 g) cornstarch

¼ tsp salt

1¼ cups (270 g) whole milk

½ tsp vanilla extract

MODELING CHOCOLATE: Though cup measurements are provided, it is highly advised that these ingredients be measured by weight. In a heatproof bowl, add the white chocolate candy wafers. Microwave and stir them in 30-second intervals, until the chocolate is melted. Set it aside.

To a separate small bowl, add the corn syrup and microwave it for 7 seconds. Do not exceed 7 seconds or the syrup will burn. Pour the corn syrup into the chocolate and gently fold it in with a rubber spatula until a lumpy dough begins to form. Avoid overmixing because the mixture will start to leach out grease.

Transfer the chocolate dough onto a plastic wrap–lined plate, cover with plastic wrap and push it down into a disk. Let the mixture cool for 45 minutes to 1 hour, until it firms up.

SAGE CREAM FILLING PART 1: In a medium saucepan, add the butter and chopped sage. Cook on medium heat until the butter begins to simmer and foam up, about 3 minutes. Don't leave it for any longer or the butter will brown. Transfer the sage butter to a round pie plate and place it in the freezer for 15 minutes to firm up a bit. Remove it from the freezer, give it a whisk and set it out on the counter until needed.

In a medium saucepan, whisk together the sugar, cornstarch and salt. Add the milk and vanilla and stir to combine. Over medium heat, stir the mixture constantly with a rubber spatula until it thickens into a pudding-like consistency. Remove it from the heat and spread the mixture in a thin layer on a large dinner plate. Cover with plastic wrap, making sure it touches the surface. Let it sit at room temperature for about 45 minutes, until it has cooled completely and congealed. Meanwhile, prepare the cookies.

(continued)

Pumpkin Cookies

⅓ cup (75 g) unsalted butter

3 cups (375 g) all-purpose flour

½ tsp baking soda

1½ tsp (7 g) baking powder

1 tsp kosher salt

2 tbsp (11 g) pumpkin pie spice

1 (15-oz [425-g]) can pumpkin puree

1 cup (200 g) granulated sugar

½ cup (110 g) light brown sugar

⅓ cup (65 g) vegetable oil

2 large eggs

½ tbsp (7 g) vanilla extract

Special Tools

Piping bag

Large piping tip

fig. 1

PUMPKIN COOKIES: Preheat the oven to 350°F (180°C). Line a baking tray with parchment paper.

Brown the butter by adding it to a small saucepan on medium heat. Let the butter melt until it begins to bubble. At this point, stir it with a rubber spatula until the bubbles begin to die down and it starts to brown. It will have a toasted aroma. Scrape it into a small bowl and set it aside.

In a medium mixing bowl, whisk together the flour, baking soda, baking powder, salt and pumpkin pie spice and set aside. In a large mixing bowl, whisk together the canned pumpkin puree and browned butter until combined. Add both sugars and mix. Lastly, add the oil, eggs and vanilla and whisk until incorporated. Sift in half of the dry mixture and fold it in with a rubber spatula until there is no more flour visible. Add the second half of the dry mixture and fold it in until just combined. Avoid mixing until it is smooth or the cookies may turn out tough. Wrap the bowl with plastic wrap and freeze the batter for 45 minutes to an hour to thicken up a bit.

With a cookie scoop, about 2 tablespoons (30 g) big, scoop the batter onto the baking tray 1 inch (2.5 cm) apart from each other. Make sure to get the scoops as round as possible. Bake for 12 to 15 minutes, until a toothpick inserted into the center comes out clean. Immediately create pumpkin ridges by gently pressing the side of a wooden skewer across the cookie, creating indents (fig. 1). Let them cool on the pan for 10 minutes before transferring to a wire rack to cool.

SAGE CREAM FILLING PART 2: This next part can be done with a hand or stand mixer, but a stand mixer with the whisk attachment will cut the time in half. Beat the sage butter for 3 minutes, until fluffy. With the mixer still running, spoon the congealed mixture into the butter, one spoonful at a time, making sure to beat well after each addition. Once all the mixture is added, beat for 5 more minutes, until creamy and no jelly bits remain. Add it to a piping bag with a large piping tip of your choosing.

☞ *The congealed mixture must be completely cooled before adding it to the butter, and the butter must be soft but not too soft. If the butter is too soft, the cream will become soupy.*

fig. 2

ASSEMBLY: Pipe the cream onto the flat side of a cookie and sandwich it with another cookie, making sure to line up the ridges.

For the stems, knead the modeling chocolate on a cold surface until it is smooth and workable. Dye half of the dough with a small amount of food dye and knead it until the desired color is reached. A mixture of browns, greens and yellows should do. Sculpt the chocolate into whimsical twisting stems and add them to the top of the cookies (fig. 2). Alternatively, an almond can be added to the top and they will be just as charming. Store any leftovers in an airtight container in the refrigerator for 2 to 3 days.

PEEK-A-BOO DELIGHTS

(CHOCOLATE & RASPBERRY)

PEEK-A-BOO, EYE SEE YOU! A TREAT WITH A MOST PECULIAR VIEW. WITH RASPBERRY JAM AND CHOCOLATE BETWEEN, THESE TRUFFLE-LIKE HEARTS WILL NOT GO UNSEEN.

Yield: 30 *sandwich cookies*

15 maraschino cherries

Ganache Filling
¾ cup + 1 tbsp (163 g) semi-sweet chocolate chips
⅓ cup + ½ tbsp (82 g) heavy whipping cream

Spritz Cookies
1 cup (226 g/2 sticks) unsalted butter, softened
½ cup + 1 tbsp (113 g) granulated sugar
1 large egg
2 tsp (8 g) vanilla extract
4 drops pink gel food dye
2½ cups (313 g) all-purpose flour
¾ tsp kosher salt
Raspberry preserves, for filling

Preheat the oven to 400°F (200°C).

Cut the maraschino cherries in half and place them cut side down on a few paper towels to remove the excess moisture. Set them aside.

GANACHE FILLING: Add the chocolate chips to a bowl. In a microwave-safe measuring cup, heat the heavy cream in the microwave in four 15-second intervals, until the temperature reaches 180°F (82°C). Pour the cream over the chocolate and cover the bowl with plastic wrap for 10 minutes. After it has sat, stir until all the chocolate is melted through. If there are still large lumps of chocolate, microwave it in 10-second intervals. Set it aside to firm up to a spreadable consistency. Meanwhile, prepare the cookies.

SPRITZ COOKIES: With an electric mixer, cream the butter and sugar together until combined. Add the egg, vanilla and pink food dye and beat until incorporated. Sift in the flour and salt, then fold it in with a rubber spatula until the dough is soft and workable.

Scoop out about ½ cup (80 g) of the dough, add it to a piping bag and set it aside. Stuff the cookie press with the larger portion of dough and attach the heart-shape cutter. Press the cookies directly onto an ungreased baking tray in four rows across. Add the halved cherries to the center of the hearts in rows 1 and 3. Those will be the top of the cookies.

Cut a hole in the piping bag and pipe eyelids around the tops and bottoms of the cherries; they won't be perfect right away. The piping bag is just an easy way to add the dough to the cookie. Use a finger and a sculpting tool to smooth and shape the eyelids. In rows 2 and 4, gently press the heart cookies down to match the size of the ones with cherry eyes.

(continued)

Royal Icing

½ cup + 1 tbsp (68 g) powdered sugar

1 tsp lemon juice

½ tbsp (7 g) whole milk

3 drops black food dye

Piping gel

Special Tools

Cookie press with heart cutter

Sculpting tool

Piping bags

If the dough is to thick to pipe, sculpt the lids manually by adding small portions around the eyes.

Bake the cookies for 6 to 8 minutes. Remove them from the oven and transfer to a wire rack to cool.

ASSEMBLY: If the ganache hasn't hardened yet, place it in the freezer in 5-minute intervals, stirring between each. Watch it like a hawk because it hardens quickly. It should firm up to a pipeable consistency like frosting. Add the ganache to a piping bag and pipe a border on the back of a bottom cookie. Fill the center with a little bit of raspberry preserves and sandwich it with a cherry eye cookie on top. Repeat for all the cookies.

ROYAL ICING: Make the black icing by combining the powdered sugar, lemon juice, milk and 3 drops of black food dye until smooth. Add it to a piping bag and snip a tiny hole at the tip. Pipe a line of icing in the center of the cherries to imitate snake eyes. Use a toothpick to control the shape of the line. Apply black icing around the eye just like applying eyeliner. Let the icing dry. Once dry, pipe a layer of piping gel on top to highlight the eyes. Display these eye-conic cookies in a candy box for the perfect Valentine's gift.

LAVENDER GEMS

Yield: 30 *cookies*

....

COOKIE DOUGH CRUSHED
BENEATH A GLASS, MOLDING
ELEGANCE WITH EVERY PASS.

PERFUMED WITH LAVENDER
AND SOFT AS SKY, SWEET LITTLE
GEMS, A FEAST FOR THE EYES.

Lavender Dough

2 cups (250 g) all-purpose flour, plus more for dusting

¼ cup (40 g) cornstarch

¼ tsp kosher salt

1 tsp dried lavender buds

¾ cup (170 g/1½ sticks) unsalted butter, softened

1 cup (113 g) powdered sugar

1 large egg

1 tsp vanilla extract

Lavender Sugar

½ tsp dried lavender buds

½ cup (100 g) granulated sugar

Glaze

¾ cup (90 g) powdered sugar, plus more if needed

½ tbsp (7 g) unsalted butter, melted

¼ tsp vanilla extract

2 tbsp (30 g) warm water, plus more if needed

1 drop purple gel food dye

Special Tools

Cut-crystal drinking glass

Mortar and pestle

Pastry brush

Gather your favorite cut-crystal or glass goblets. The ones that work best have intricate designs on the bottom of them. Though glasses like this look expensive, they can easily be found for a bargain at thrift shops or for free if one dares to raid their grandmother's china cabinet.

LAVENDER DOUGH: In a small bowl, whisk together the flour, cornstarch and salt. Set it aside. Grind the lavender into a powder with a mortar and pestle. Add it to a large bowl along with the butter and powdered sugar. Beat for 1 minute, until creamy. Add the egg and vanilla and beat for 1 more minute. Add half of the dry ingredients and mix on low speed until just combined, making sure not to overmix. Add the last bit of dry ingredients and finish mixing by hand with a rubber spatula until combined. The dough will be sticky.

Dump the dough onto plastic wrap, cover it and pat it into a thin disk. Chill in the refrigerator for 2 hours to firm up. Meanwhile, prepare the lavender sugar and glaze.

LAVENDER SUGAR: Grind the lavender buds into a powder with a mortar and pestle. Sift it into a bowl with the sugar to remove any large pieces and mix. Set it aside.

GLAZE: In a small bowl, whisk together the powdered sugar, melted butter, vanilla and warm water until the mixture is a thin, runny consistency. If it is too thin, add 1 tablespoon (7 g) more of powdered sugar. If it's too thick, add 1 teaspoon more of water. Mix in a drop of purple food dye. Cover the bowl with plastic wrap to prevent the glaze from drying out and set it aside.

Preheat the oven to 350°F (180°C) and line two baking trays with parchment paper. The baking trays should be able to fit in your freezer.

(continued)

fig. 1 fig. 2

LAVENDER GEMS *continued*

ASSEMBLY: Remove the dough from the refrigerator. Measure out a tablespoon-size of dough, roll it into a ball and set it on a plate. Continue with the remainder of the dough. Lightly flour a clean surface. Roll a dough ball in the lavender sugar to coat it evenly, then place it on the floured surface.

Dip the bottom of a cut-crystal glass in flour, then gently press it onto the dough ball to flatten it until it is the diameter of the glass (fig. 1). Lift the glass up. If it sticks to the dough, gently peel it off. Turn the glass over onto the dough and shake the glass in a circular motion for a few seconds to smooth out the edges (fig. 2).

Use a spatula to transfer the cookie to the baking tray. Continue the process with the rest of the dough balls. The trick to successful cookie shaping is to have the surface lightly floured so the cookie can move freely when shaping the edges. If the cookie dough sticks to the surface during the edge shaping step, it will become thick and deformed.

Once all the cookies have been formed, place the trays in the freezer for 20 minutes to firm up. This will help them keep their shape while baking. Once chilled, bake for 9 to 11 minutes. As soon as the cookies come out of the oven, use a pastry brush to brush them with the glaze, then let them cool on the pan. Once the icing hardens, enjoy with a cup of tea. Store these gems in an airtight container for 3 to 5 days.

CINNAMON LIME SKELETONS

CINNAMON AND LIME, AN UNLIKELY PAIR. THESE SWEET LITTLE BONES MAY GIVE YOU A SCARE. SOFT AND QUITE FRAGILE, THESE SKELETONS ARE A MIXTURE OF FLAVORS THAT'S TRULY BIZARRE.

Yield: 9 skeletons

Skeleton Dough

2⅔ cups (335 g) all-purpose flour, plus more for dusting

2 tbsp (20 g) cornstarch

½ tsp kosher salt

1½ tsp (4 g) cinnamon

2 tbsp (14 g) black cocoa powder

1 cup (226 g/2 sticks) unsalted butter, softened

½ cup (110 g) brown sugar

½ cup (60 g) powdered sugar

1½ tsp (3 g) lime zest (about 3 limes)

2 tbsp (30 g) lime juice

1 egg

1 tsp vanilla extract

6 drops black food dye

Royal Icing

1 cup + 2 tbsp (134 g) powdered sugar

2 tsp (9 g) lime juice

1 tbsp (15 g) pasteurized carton egg whites or whole milk (see Note)

Special Tools

Embossed skeleton cookie cutter or gingerbread man cutter

Piping bag

Piping tip (Wilton #3)

Cookie spatula

SKELETON DOUGH: In a medium bowl, whisk the flour, cornstarch, salt, cinnamon and black cocoa powder until combined. Set it aside.

In a large bowl with an electric mixer, cream together the butter, brown sugar, powdered sugar and lime zest until fluffy, about 3 minutes. Scrape down the sides of the bowl, then add the lime juice, egg, vanilla and black food dye. Beat for 30 more seconds, until combined. On low speed, slowly add the dry ingredients until the dough begins to form—do not overmix. The dough will be soft and sticky. Wrap the dough in plastic wrap and refrigerate for 4 to 6 hours to firm up. Preheat the oven to 350°F (180°C) and line two baking trays with parchment paper.

Roll the cookie dough out on a lightly floured surface. With an embossed skeleton cookie cutter, cut out the shapes in the dough. Remove the excess dough and scoop the cookies up with a wide cookie spatula. Transfer them to the parchment-lined baking tray. If the dough gets too soft, place it in the freezer for 10 minutes.

Bake for 15 to 17 minutes, until they are just set so they don't dry out. Let them cool on the pan for 10 minutes before gently transferring them to a wire rack to cool.

ROYAL ICING: Mix the powdered sugar, lime juice and pasteurized egg whites until smooth and shiny. Immediately place the icing into a piping bag with a Wilton #3 piping tip to keep it from drying out. Decorate each cookie bone by bone, then let them dry. Store them in an airtight container for 3 to 4 days.

Pasteurized egg whites from a carton are safe to eat raw because they have been heat treated like milk. If you are still wary of consuming them, you may substitute 1 tablespoon (15 g) of whole milk, but this will take longer to dry.

LOVE SPELL COOKIES

(ROSE, CARDAMOM & PISTACHIO)

ROSES ARE DEAD, CARDAMOM'S SWEET, PISTACHIOS ARE CRUNCHY AND SO GOOD TO EAT. A MIXTURE OF FLAVORS WRAPPED UP SO WELL, WILL CONJURE A CLEVER AND DECADENT SPELL.

Yield: **14** *cookies*

Cookie Dough

1 cup (120 g) shelled, roasted pistachios, divided, plus more for garnish

2¾ cups (344 g) all-purpose flour

1 tbsp (10 g) cornstarch

½ tsp baking powder

½ tsp baking soda

1 tsp cardamom

½ tsp nutmeg

½ tsp kosher salt

1 cup (213 g) brown sugar

⅓ cup (67 g) granulated sugar

14 tbsp (198 g) unsalted butter, melted and cooled

1 tbsp (12 g) olive oil

1 large egg

1 large egg yolk

2 tsp (10 g) rose water (see Note)

¼ tsp vanilla extract

¼ cup (3 g) dried culinary rose buds, crushed, plus more for garnish

Rose Drizzle

1¼ cups (150 g) powdered sugar

2 tsp (10 g) rose water

1 tbsp (15 g) milk

2 drops pink food dye

Rose water can be found at most grocery stores in the Middle Eastern food section.

COOKIE DOUGH: Roughly chop the pistachios. Set ½ cup (60 g) aside. To a food processor, finely pulverize the remaining ½ cup (60 g) of pistachios until it looks like coarse sand. Dump it into a small bowl and set it aside.

In a medium bowl, whisk together the flour, cornstarch, baking powder, baking soda, cardamom, nutmeg and salt. Set it aside. In a large bowl, whisk together both sugars, the melted butter, olive oil, egg, egg yolk, rose water and vanilla until smooth. Add the dry ingredients and fold it in with a rubber spatula until a dough forms. Add in the ½ cup (60 g) of roughly chopped pistachios and crushed rose petals. Gently mix until dispersed. Cover the bowl with plastic wrap and freeze for 30 minutes.

Once chilled, using a ¼-cup (60-ml) cookie scoop, scoop the dough into your palm and lightly roll it into individual balls. Roll the dough balls in the ground pistachios to coat them and place them on a parchment-lined baking tray. Lightly press the cookies down to flatten the top. They should be about ¾ inch (2 cm) thick. All the cookies should fit on one baking sheet. Chill them in the freezer for 30 minutes.

After 15 minutes, preheat the oven to 350°F (180°C) and line a baking sheet with parchment paper. Place the dough balls 2 inches (5 cm) apart. Bake for 15 to 17 minutes, until the sides are set and the centers look a bit underdone. Cool them completely on the pan for about 1 hour. The trick to getting these cookies to be soft and chewy in the center is to take them out when the centers are a little underbaked. Cooling them on the pan helps them set up because the heat of the pan will continue to gently bake them.

ROSE DRIZZLE: Whisk together the powdered sugar, rose water, milk and pink food dye until smooth. Pour the mixture into a piping bag and drizzle over the cooled cookies. Quickly sprinkle crushed roses and pistachios for garnish. Once the icing has dried, the spell is complete and they're ready to eat! Store them in an airtight container for 3 to 5 days.

Peachy Oat-Mealworm Cookies

Chewy oat cookies, a peachy delight. Mealworms crawling on every bite.

Yield: *8 cookies*

....

Modeling Chocolate Mealworms

1 (12-oz [350-g]) bag white melting chocolate candy wafers

¼ cup (84 g) light corn syrup

Gel food dye (yellow, brown, orange)

1 drop vanilla extract

Peach Filling

1 (15-oz [425-g]) can yellow cling sliced peaches (reserve the juice)

3 tbsp (42 g) dark brown sugar

¼ tsp ground cardamom

⅛ tsp ground cinnamon

A pinch of salt

1 tbsp (10 g) cornstarch

MODELING CHOCOLATE: Though cup measurements are provided, it is highly advised that these ingredients be measured by weight for the most accurate result. In a heat-proof bowl, add the white chocolate candy wafers. Microwave and stir in 30-second intervals, until the chocolate is melted. Set it aside.

Add the corn syrup to a separate small heatproof bowl and microwave for 7 seconds—do not exceed 7 seconds or the syrup will burn. Pour the corn syrup into the chocolate and gently fold it in with a rubber spatula just until a lumpy dough begins to form. Don't mix any further or the mixture will start to leach out grease.

Transfer the chocolate dough onto a plastic wrap–lined plate, cover with plastic wrap and push it down into a disk. Let the mixture cool for 45 minutes to 1 hour, until it firms up. Meanwhile, prepare the filling.

PEACH FILLING: Strain the can of peaches over a bowl to catch the juice. Set the juice aside for later and chop the peaches into ½-inch (1.3-cm) chunks. Add them to a medium pot along with the brown sugar, cardamom, cinnamon and salt. Cook on medium heat until the sugar melts and the mixture begins to simmer, about 5 minutes.

In a small bowl, mix 2 tablespoons (30 g) of the reserved peach juice and the cornstarch to create a slurry. Pour it into the simmering peaches and mix until it thickens. Don't overcook the peaches or else they will become too mushy. Transfer the filling to a dinner plate and spread it into a thin layer to cool. Meanwhile, prepare the cookie dough.

(continued)

Cookie Dough

1¼ cups (156 g) all-purpose flour, plus more for dusting

¾ cup (75 g) whole rolled oats

1 tbsp (10 g) cornstarch

½ tsp baking soda

¼ tsp ground cinnamon

½ tsp kosher salt

½ cup (113 g) unsalted butter, softened

1 tbsp (14 g) vegetable oil

½ cup + 2 tbsp (130 g) dark brown sugar

1 large egg

1 tsp vanilla extract

¾ cup (95 g) toasted pecans, chopped

1 egg white + 1 tsp cold water, for brushing

Cinnamon Drizzle

¼ cup (30 g) powdered sugar, plus more if needed

¼ tsp cinnamon

1 tsp milk, plus more if needed

Special Tools

Clean hair comb (new)

Piping bag

Small paintbrush

COOKIE DOUGH: In a medium bowl, whisk together the flour, oats, cornstarch, baking soda, cinnamon and salt. Set it aside.

In a large bowl, beat the butter, vegetable oil and brown sugar for 2 minutes, until fluffy. Add the egg and vanilla and beat for an additional 30 seconds. Fold in the dry ingredients with a rubber spatula until halfway mixed, then add in the toasted pecans and mix just until combined, making sure not to overmix. The dough will be soft. Cover the bowl with plastic wrap and refrigerate for 30 minutes so it can firm up a bit.

Meanwhile, line three baking trays with parchment paper. One will be used for chilling and the other two will be used for baking. Once the dough has firmed up, use a ¼ cup–sized cookie scoop or measuring cup to scoop out eight balls of dough. Place them on a baking tray. They don't have to be spaced out too far apart at this point. Slightly flatten the cookies with the palm of your hand, so they look like hockey pucks and are roughly ¾ inch (2 cm) thick. Dip the back of a rounded measuring spoon that is a tablespoon in size into flour. Use the bottom to press down into the center of each cookie to make a deep indentation. If the dough cracks around the ends while pushing down, no worries, just sculpt the cracks back together. Freeze the dough for 15 minutes to firm up.

Preheat the oven to 410°F (210°C).

Once the cookies have firmed up, place them on the room temperature, parchment-lined baking trays. Space them about 2½ inches (6 cm) apart so they don't spread into each other during baking. Lightly whisk the egg white and cold water, then brush the tops of the cookies with a thin layer of the egg wash. Try to avoid getting any egg wash on the pan or it may burn.

Bake the cookies for 9 to 11 minutes, just until the centers start to firm up. Remove the baking trays from the oven and re-indent the middle with the measuring spoon. Let them cool completely on the trays. The cookies will look a bit underbaked in the center, but they will continue to cook and firm up as they cool on the trays. This method helps to keep the cookies soft and chewy.

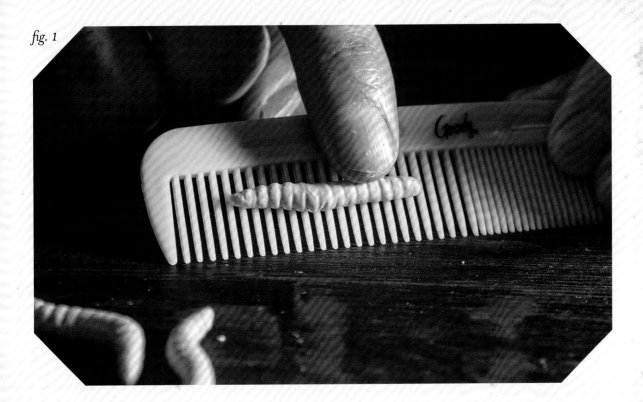

fig. 1

To make the cookies rounder, place a hot cookie that's right out of the oven on a cutting board. Place a small bowl upside-down over the cookie and shake the bowl in a circular motion. As the bowl is moving, the cookie will hit the sides of it and will become round. Immediately place the cookie back on the hot pan to cool. Do this one cookie at a time.

CINNAMON DRIZZLE: Whisk together the powdered sugar, cinnamon and milk until a drizzle consistency is achieved. If the mixture is too dry, and a few drops of milk; if too wet, add a bit more powdered sugar. Place the icing into a piping bag and cut a small hole at the tip. Drizzle the icing in thin threads over the cookies. Carefully spoon the peach mixture onto the center of each cookie.

MEALWORMS: Knead a quarter of the modeling chocolate to loosen it up into a clay consistency. Using a toothpick, add teeny tiny amounts of brown, yellow and orange food dye. Knead it into the modeling chocolate until you create a color similar to mealworms. Be sure to use the food dye sparingly. A little goes a long way. You can always add more color, but you cannot subtract. Once the desired color is achieved, pinch off a pea-sized amount of modeling chocolate and roll it into a mealworm shape.

Starting at the top of a comb, roll the chocolate mealworms down to create ridges (fig. 1). Place them on a piece of parchment paper. Make 24 mealworms. Mix a small drop of vanilla extract with a small drop of brown food dye to create a watery, edible paint. With a small paintbrush, paint each tip of the mealworms brown. Add them to the tops of the cookies, and BAM! Perfect Peach Oat-Mealworm Cookies. They're perfect for spring.

Store these in an airtight container in the refrigerator for up to 2 days.

BISCOCHITOS

(ANISE, CINNAMON & SUGAR)

Yield: 2 dozen cookies

....

Dough

¾ tsp (3 g) anise seeds

3 cups (375 g) all-purpose flour, plus more dusting

1 tsp (4 g) baking powder

¼ tsp kosher salt (see note)

1 cup (215 g) lard (no substitutions; I used Morrell® Snow Cap. Lard)

¾ cups (150 g) granulated sugar

2 tsp (8 g) anise extract

1 large egg, room temperature

1½ tsp (7 g) vanilla extract

1 tbsp (14 g) brandy

Topping

½ cup (100 g) granulated sugar

2 tsp (6 g) ground cinnamon

> These cookies were my first introduction to the world of baking. I would help my grandma bake hundreds of them every holiday. Traditionally, they are prepared with lard. Any other substitutions change the cookie drastically. In this adaptation, adding both ground anise seeds and anise extract amp up the warm licorice flavor in this New Mexican classic.

> A COOKIE I HOLD NEAR AND DEAR, BAKED BY MY GRANDMA EVERY YEAR. A RECIPE CONJURED AGES AGO BY FAMILIES OF NEW MEXICO. TAKEN FROM THE WINTER'S SHELF, ENCHANTING AS THE LAND ITSELF. ITS FLAKY TEXTURE AND ANISE DOUGH IS PERFECT FOR THE WINTER SNOW.

Preheat the oven to 350°F (180°F).

With a mortar and pestle, grind the anise seeds along with 1 teaspoon of the sugar until it turns into a powder. Set it aside. In a medium bowl combine the flour, baking powder and salt. Whisk it together and set it aside. In a large bowl, add the lard, sugar, the ground anise sugar and anise extract.

With one hand, knead the lard into the sugar until it combines into a mass. Add the egg, vanilla extract and brandy. Knead the ingredients together for a bit, then form your hand in a claw position and mix vigorously, as if using a whisk, for 45 seconds, until the mixture is well combined. Add in the dry mixture and gently knead until the dough forms. There should be no residue left on the sides of the bowl. Cover the bowl with a tea towel and let it rest for 15 minutes.

👉 *Use ⅛ teaspoon of salt if using regular table salt.*

Meanwhile, prepare the topping in a large plate, mix the sugar and cinnamon with a fork and set it aside.

Line two baking sheets with parchment paper. Working with half the dough, roll it out on a lightly floured surface to ¼-inch (6-mm) thickness. Cut out with your desired cookie cutter shape. Basic shapes work the best. Remove the excess dough around the cookies. Lift the cookies from the surface and plop them face down into the cinnamon sugar topping. Lightly pat the cookie down into the topping and place it sugar side up on a parchment-lined baking sheet. Bake the cookies for 10 to 12 minutes, rotating halfway through, until the bottoms are golden brown. Transfer the cookies to a cooling rack. These cookies get more flavorful the more they age. They will last up to 1 month in an airtight tin.

KEY LIME CRISPS

Yield: 4 dozen crisps

....

1 tsp lime zest
¼ cup (50 g) granulated sugar
1 large egg white
¼ tsp kosher salt
½ cup (50 g) almond flour
1 tbsp (8 g) all-purpose flour
Gold luster dust

Special Tools
Key template (page 177)
Piping tip (Wilton #3)
Soft blush makeup brush (see Note)

Preheat the oven to 350°F (180°C). Print out the key template and place it onto a large baking sheet. Cut a sheet of parchment paper to fit the cookie sheet and place it on top of the template so that the keys show through.

Chop the lime zest into small bits, then rub the zest into the sugar with your fingers to release its oils and set it aside. To a medium mixing bowl, add the egg white and whisk until foamy, soft peaks form. While whisking, gradually sprinkle in the lime sugar and salt. The mixture should turn shiny and thick while still being able to flow off the whisk. Sift in the almond and all-purpose flour and fold it in with a rubber spatula. Once combined, it should resemble a thick batter. Add it to a piping bag with a Wilton #3 piping tip.

☞ *To prevent a mess, place the empty piping bag in a tall glass and fold the sides over before adding the mixture.*

Pipe the mixture onto the parchment-covered key template. Follow the lines as closely as possible. If the lines aren't straight, use a toothpick to clean the sides up. If the piping bag gets clogged with lime zest, stick a toothpick in the tip to unclog it.

Once the keys have been piped, gently remove the key template from under the parchment paper. Bake at 350°F (180°C) for 6 to 8 minutes, until crispy. After cooling for 1 minute, immediately brush the keys with gold luster dust while on the pan.

☞ *The best method is to use a new blush makeup brush to apply the luster dust. Adding the luster dust while the cookies are still hot and pliable will help keep them from breaking.*

After dusting, let the cookies cool on the pan completely to crisp up. To remove the cookies from the pan, slide the parchment paper with the cookies onto a flat surface and use an offset spatula to carefully remove the keys.

It is said that "nothing gold can stay," and that's true for these cookies. They are best when eaten the same day. If they are left out uncovered, they will soften and become flimsy. This can be avoided by storing them in an airtight container; or, they can be re-crisped in the oven at 350°F (180°C) for 3 to 5 minutes.

PIÑON COOKIES

(PINE NUTS & JUNIPER)

Yield: 30 (4-inch [10-cm]) pinecones

....

Juniper Sugar

1 tsp juniper berries

2 tbsp (25 g) granulated sugar

Piñon Dough

¼ cup (36 g) pine nuts

1¾ cups (220 g) all-purpose flour

½ tsp baking powder

¼ tsp kosher salt

½ cup (113 g/1 stick) unsalted butter, softened

½ cup (110 g) dark brown sugar

1 large egg, room temperature

½ tbsp (11 g) raw honey

½ tsp vanilla extract

Cooking oil

Powdered sugar, for dusting

Special Tools

Mortar and pestle

Wooden pinecone cookie mold

JUNIPER SUGAR: In a mortar and pestle, add the juniper berries and sugar. Grind it up until the juniper has dispersed though the sugar into small pieces. Sift the sugar through a sieve and grind any remaining juniper berries as small as possible.

PIÑON DOUGH: To toast the pine nuts, add them to a dry pan over medium heat. Stir them constantly until fragrant, about 3 minutes. Dump them on a plate to cool. Once cooled, pulse them in a food processor until it looks like coarse sand. Alternatively, the nuts can be finely chopped into exceedingly small pieces.

☛ *Avoid processing the nuts while they are hot, or they will turn into a paste.*

In a medium bowl, whisk together the flour, ground pine nuts, baking powder and salt. Set it aside.

In a large bowl, cream the butter, brown sugar and juniper sugar for 5 minutes, until light and fluffy. Add the egg, honey and vanilla and beat until combined. Add the dry ingredients and fold it in with a rubber spatula until a dough forms. Cover it in plastic wrap and refrigerate for 4 hours or overnight for the dough to stiffen and the flavors to meld. The longer the dough chills, the easier it is to get it out of the wooden mold. While the dough is chilling, read ahead to learn how to season a new wooden mold for molding.

WOODEN COOKIE MOLDS: Wooden cookie molds can be traced back to medieval times. Craftsmen would carve out various designs by hand. Cookie dough was then pressed into the crevasses and peeled away to reveal magical patterns. These molds are still made today and can be purchased online in a variety of designs. Making cookies with a wooden mold does have its challenges. Having patience with the technique will yield the most beautiful cookies.

(continued)

PIÑON COOKIES *continued*

HOW TO USE A WOODEN COOKIE MOLD: Like cast-iron cookware, new wooden cookie molds need to be seasoned. This helps the cookie dough release from the mold easier. Brush the mold with cooking oil and wipe it off with a paper towel. Let it sit for a few hours for the wood to absorb the oil.

Once the dough has chilled, dry brush a generous amount of flour into the cookie mold and lightly tap out any excess. The trick to getting a clean release is to use enough flour. Take a small bit of the chilled dough and lightly press it into the mold. Use a rolling pin to roll over the back. Cut the excess dough with a sharp knife in a light sawing motion. Pull the dough away from the edges of the mold (fig. 1). Hit the corner of the mold on your work surface a few times until the dough falls out. Don't be afraid to use force (fig. 2). Dust off the excess flour with a pastry brush (fig. 3).

With an offset spatula, transfer the molded cookies onto a parchment-lined baking tray. Continue with the rest of the dough until it is all used up. Remember to generously dust the mold with flour between each cookie. If the dough gets too soft, stick it in the freezer for 15 minutes. Once all the cookies have been molded, place them in the freezer for 15 minutes to firm up.

Meanwhile, preheat the oven to 350°F (180°C) and line a baking sheet with parchment paper. Once the cookies are firm, place them on the parchment-lined, room-temperature baking sheet 1 inch (2.5 cm) apart. Bake for 15 to 18 minutes, until the edges are golden brown. Transfer the cookies to a wire rack to cool completely.

Once cooled, sprinkle the cookies with a light dusting of powdered sugar by placing the pinecones standing up along the inside walls of a cake pan. Use a sieve to dust the powdered sugar. Dusting the cookies while standing them up gives the illusion of directional snowfall, which also highlights the pattern of the pinecone.

These cookies are a great companion to coffee. Store the leftovers in an airtight container for up to a week.

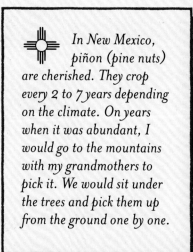

In New Mexico, piñon (pine nuts) are cherished. They crop every 2 to 7 years depending on the climate. On years when it was abundant, I would go to the mountains with my grandmothers to pick it. We would sit under the trees and pick them up from the ground one by one.

fig. 1

fig. 2

fig. 3

Chewy Cobweb Brownies

Sweetest of webs spun by icing. A thick, chewy brownie that's quite enticing. Chocolaty bliss, these decadent blocks are far better than what comes in the box. Easy as pie, only one bowl required. Baking a batch will leave you "inspidered."

Yield: 9 brownies

Brownie Batter

¾ cup (170 g/1½ sticks) unsalted butter

1½ cups (300 g) granulated sugar

¼ cup (55 g) brown sugar

½ cup + 2 tbsp (58 g) Dutch-processed cocoa powder

¼ cup (56 g) vegetable oil

3 large eggs, room temperature

1 tbsp (13 g) vanilla extract

1 tsp instant espresso powder

1¼ cups (156 g) all-purpose flour

⅛ tsp baking soda

1 tsp kosher salt

1 tbsp (10 g) cornstarch

Cobweb Icing

1¾ cups (210 g) powdered sugar, plus more if needed

1 tsp lemon juice, plus more if needed

2 tbsp (30 g) pasteurized egg whites in a carton or whole milk, plus more if needed

Special Tools

Piping bag

Preheat the oven to 325°F (165°C). Line an 8 x 8–inch (20 x 20–cm) square pan with parchment paper. Spray it with nonstick baking spray and set it aside.

BROWNIE BATTER: In a large microwave-safe bowl, add the butter and both sugars. Microwave for 1 minute in 15-second intervals, stirring with a rubber spatula between each interval. Once the butter is melted into the sugar, sift in the cocoa powder and mix. Add the vegetable oil and mix, then add the eggs, one at a time, until just combined. Lastly, add the vanilla and espresso powder and mix until the mixture is glossy and well incorporated. Make sure to stir the ingredients in a gentle motion to avoid trapping major air bubbles in the batter. Sift in the flour, baking soda, salt and cornstarch. Mix in a folding motion for 20 to 25 folds, or until a thick, glossy batter is achieved—do not overmix.

Spread the batter evenly into the parchment-lined square pan. Bake for 45 to 50 minutes, until the top and sides have set and a toothpick comes out mostly clean when inserted into the center. Let the brownies cool in the pan completely for 2 hours before cutting.

COBWEB ICING: Once the brownies have cooled, prepare the cobweb icing by mixing the powdered sugar, lemon juice and pasteurized egg whites in a bowl until thick and glossy. The consistency should be of thick glue. It should be thick enough to hold its shape when piped. If the icing is too thin, add 1 tablespoon (8 g) more of powdered sugar. If it's too thick, add a few drops more of lemon juice.

Lift the brownies out of the pan using the parchment paper and cut them into even squares. Add the icing to a piping bag and cut the tip small enough to get a thin, even thread of icing when gently squeezed. Pipe a spiderweb pattern on each of the squares, using the photo as a reference, and let it dry. Enjoy with a glass of milk. These brownies can be stored in an airtight container at room temperature for up to a week.

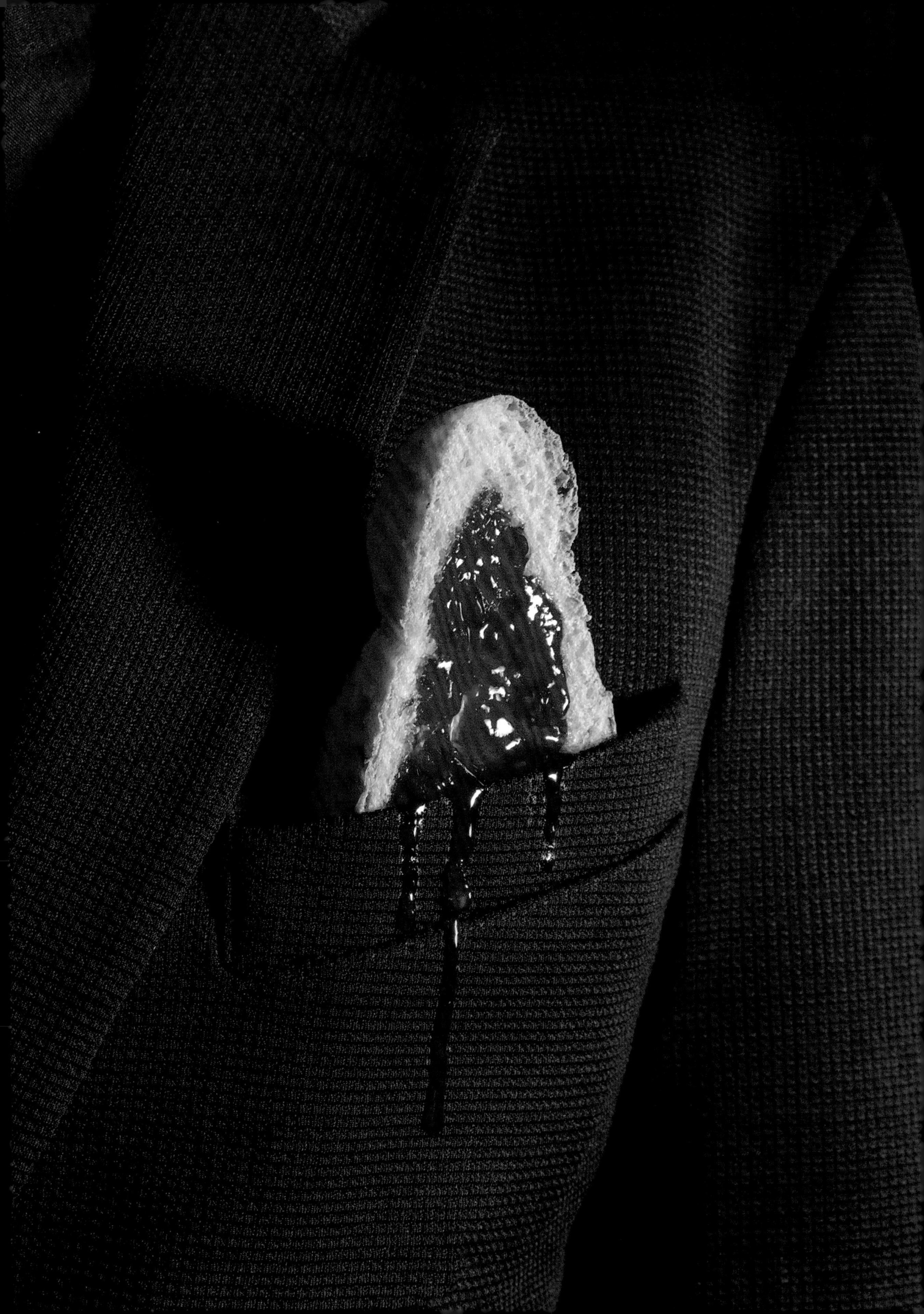

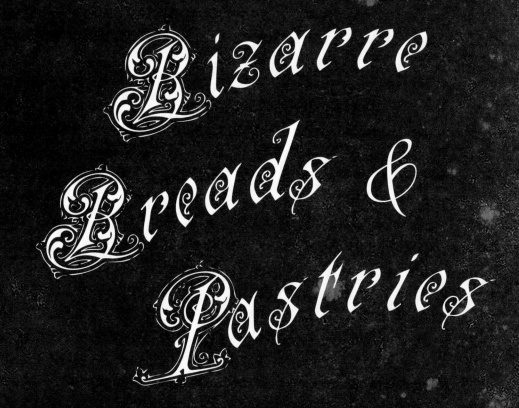

Bizarre Breads & Pastries

"THE RISE TO THE OCCASION... LITERALLY."

BREAD BASICS

Bread is pure magic. It requires four elements to yield an amazing final product:

- ☞ Earth = flour and salt
- ☞ Water = liquid ingredients
- ☞ Air = yeast
- ☞ Fire = the oven.

Here are some best practices to make sure your bread doesn't backfire.

Measuring Bread Ingredients: Bread can be quite finicky. Especially if the ingredients are measured improperly. It is highly recommended that the ingredients be measured by weight on a food scale. This will help yield the best possible final product. The bread recipes in this section are listed in gram measurements first followed by cup measurements. The cup measurements are estimated amounts. If you must measure by cups, follow the method on how to measure flour on page 10.

Flour: Bread flour and all-purpose flour are not interchangeable when making bread. Bread flour contains more protein to build gluten, which is responsible for the structure of the bread. All-purpose flour produces less of a structure because the protein percentage is lower.

Yeast and Temperature: Temperature plays a huge role in bread making because it involves yeast. Yeast is a living organism that is activated by warm liquid and feeds off of sugar. The type of yeast used in this book is active dry yeast, which activates between 105 and 110°F (40 and 43°C). Any higher and the yeast will die; any lower and the yeast won't wake up. This is why an instant-read thermometer is an essential tool for bread making.

Kneading Dough: Kneading the dough builds gluten, which is responsible for the structure and texture of bread. Some recipes in this book can be kneaded by hand and some require a stand mixer due to the stickiness of the dough.

How to Knead Dough

- ☞ On a clean surface, push the dough down and away from you with the heel of your hand.
- ☞ Fold the top of the dough over on itself and press down and outward.
- ☞ Push the dough down again and repeat, making sure to rotate the dough. The dough is sufficiently kneaded when it's smooth and passes the windowpane test on the following page.

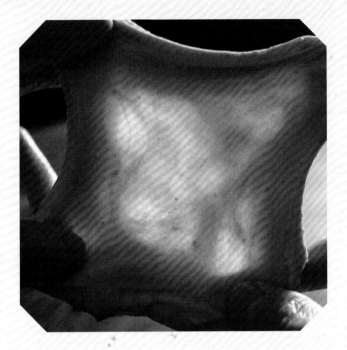

Windowpane Test

The windowpane test is a practical way of checking if the dough has been kneaded thoroughly. Cut off a small piece of dough and hold it with both hands. Slowly stretch it between your thumb and first two fingers until it becomes thin and translucent. Hold it up to the light. If the light shines through with no tears in the dough, then it has been thoroughly kneaded.

Proofing: Proofing is a crucial step of baking bread. It allows the dough to ferment and rise. Each bread recipe in this book requires two rises. It is crucial to keep track of time and temperature at these stages. For the best results, let the dough proof in a warm room to allow the yeast to work its magic. Every bread is at the mercy of the climate that it's being made in. The times and temperatures that work in my kitchen may not act the same way in your kitchen. That is why it is best to use the times that I give as a guideline. Use diligence and visual cues to determine when your bread is sufficiently proofed.

👉 **First Proof:** The initial proof/rise is the easiest because it is done after the dough is kneaded in an oiled bowl. It is usually done proofing after the dough doubles in size.

👉 **Second Proof:** The final proof/rise is crucial for bread art. This will determine the texture and shape of the final product. If left to proof for too little, the bread will become dense and can potentially distort the shape. The visual cue I use for proofing is the poke test. Flour your finger and gently press a small indent in the dough. If the dough springs back quickly, it is not ready. If the dough springs back slowly, it is ready to be baked. Additionally, if the dough does not spring back at all, the dough is overproofed.

Cooling: Cutting bread before it has cooled will result in a very gummy texture. It is still cooking as it cools. Most breads are ready to eat in an hour and a half after being baked.

A BUG-UETTE

A BUG-UETTE CRAWLS UPON THE PLATE, CREEPY LEGS IN A CRUSTY STATE. SOFT AND CHEWY, THIS BUG OF BREAD IS PERFECT WITH BUTTER, STEW AND SPREAD.

Yield: 1 *beetle loaf*

Dough

270 g (1¼ cups) water

2 tbsp (25 g) granulated sugar

12 g (1 tbsp) active dry yeast

440 g (4 cups) bread flour, sifted

28 g (2 tbsp) butter, melted, plus more for brushing

26 g (2 tbsp) vegetable shortening, melted

9 g (1½ tsp) kosher salt

☞ *Placing the bowl of dough in a microwave that is turned off is a great draft-free place to proof bread dough.*

DOUGH: Using a glass measuring cup, microwave the water in 10-second intervals, until the temperature reaches between 105 and 110°F (40 and 43°C). Add the sugar and stir until dissolved, then stir in the yeast. Let the mixture sit for 5 minutes, until it starts to foam at the surface. Meanwhile, in a large bowl, add the flour, melted butter, melted shortening and salt. Once the yeast has foamed, add it to the large bowl, making sure to scrape all the remaining yeast off the side of the cup with a rubber spatula. Mix until a mass of dough forms.

Turn it out on a lightly floured surface and knead for 10 minutes. Test the gluten development with the windowpane test (page 117). Once the dough has been sufficiently kneaded, place it in a large buttered bowl. Butter the top of the dough to avoid drying and cover it with plastic wrap. Let it rise for 1 hour in a warm and draft-free place until doubled in size.

SHAPING: Once the dough has doubled in size, lightly push it down to release the air. Dump the dough out on a lightly floured surface. Lightly flatten the dough into a 12-inch (30-cm)-long slab. Remove about 1½ inches (4 cm) of dough from one end to use for the legs later (fig. 1). Roll the dough into a log and pinch the bottom seam closed (fig. 2). Tuck the ends under the log. Transfer to a parchment-lined baking sheet.

(continued)

fig. 1

fig. 2

Egg Wash
1 egg yolk

1 tsp water

A pinch of salt

Special Tools
Bakers' twine

Pastry brush

Casserole dish

Instant-read thermometer

With scissors, cut one end down the middle about 2 inches (5 cm) down and roll them to a point to imitate the pinchers (fig. 3). Crimp the exposed dough closed that was made by the cut. Shape the back side to be a bit larger than the pincher side by folding the dough under itself. Gently tie bakers' twine around the body to separate the head, thorax and abdomen (fig. 4).

With the extra dough, form three 10-inch (25-cm)-long logs and cut them in half to get six 5-inch (13-cm)-long legs. Tuck them under the beetle. Position them in an L shape to imitate crawling (fig. 5). With scissors, gently snip the outsides of the legs to create setae (little hairs) and do the same on the inside of the pinchers. With a sharp knife, cut a line down the abdomen (fig. 6).

EGG WASH: Prepare an egg wash by whisking the egg yolk, water and a pinch of salt. Gently brush the top of the bread with the egg wash and loosely cover with plastic wrap. Let the dough rise for about 30 minutes.

Meanwhile, preheat the oven to 400°F (200°C) and place a casserole dish on the bottom wrack. Boil water in a kettle to prepare for baking.

Once the dough has doubled in size, gently brush a second coat of egg wash over it. Pour the boiling water into the casserole dish on the bottom rack of the oven. Place the bread on the top wrack and bake uninterrupted for 18 to 20 minutes. Avoid opening the oven during this time because this will disrupt the rise. After 18 minutes, test the temperature by sticking a thermometer in the center of the thorax. Once the temperature is between 205 and 210°F (90 and 95°C), it is done. Remove the bread from the oven and let sit for 5 minutes on the pan. Transfer to a cooling rack to cool completely before enjoying with butter or soup or as a sandwich.

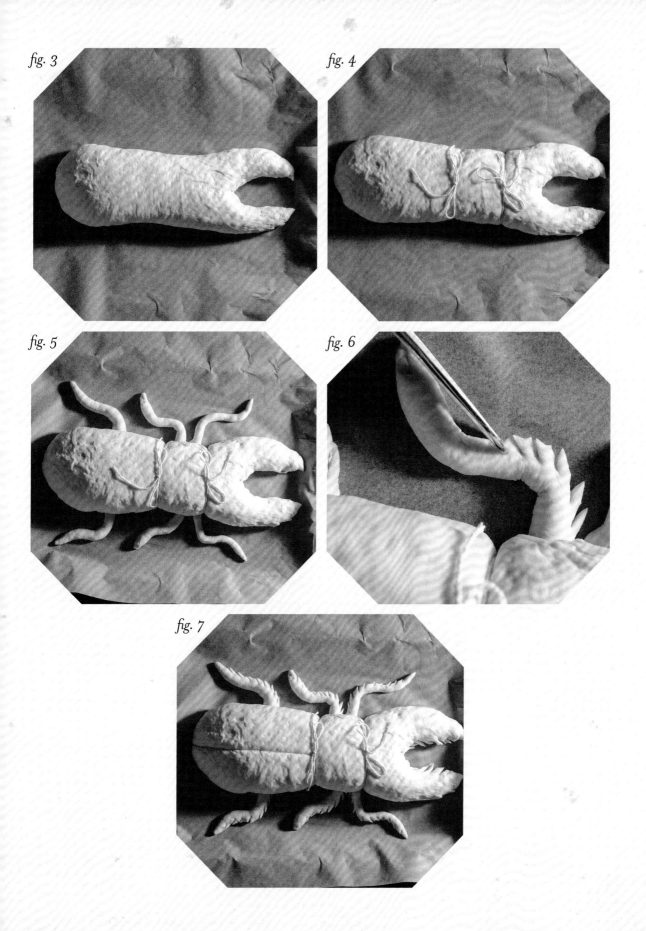

fig. 3

fig. 4

fig. 5

fig. 6

fig. 7

Mourning Buns

(PAN DULCE)

Mourning buns are a somber treat. Blackened bread with a dough so sweet. A hint of lime to wake the dead, with whom you should enjoy this bread.

Yield: 1 *dozen buns*

....

Sweet Dough

110 g (½ cup) canned evaporated milk

50 g (¼ cup) water

50 g (¼ cup) granulated sugar, divided

12 g (1 tbsp) active dry yeast

563 g (4½ cups) all-purpose flour, sifted, plus more for dusting

55 g (¼ cup) brown sugar

1 tsp kosher salt

85 g (6 tbsp) unsalted butter, melted, plus more for brushing

26 g (2 tbsp) vegetable shortening, melted

3 large eggs

1 tsp vanilla extract

Blackend Topping

85 g (6 tbsp) unsalted butter, softened

20 g (2 tbsp) vegetable shortening

135 g (1 cup) powdered sugar

141 g (1 cup) all-purpose flour

14 g (2 tbsp) black cocoa powder

¼ tsp cinnamon

13 g (3 tsp) vanilla extract

½ tsp lime zest

SWEET DOUGH: Using a glass measuring cup, microwave the evaporated milk and water in 10-second intervals, until the temperature reaches between 105 and 110°F (40 and 43°C). Add 1 teaspoon of granulated sugar and stir until dissolved, then mix in the yeast. Let the mixture sit for 5 minutes, until it starts to foam on the surface.

Meanwhile, in a large bowl, add the flour, brown sugar, granulated sugar and salt and whisk until combined. Make a well in the center and add the butter, shortening, eggs, vanilla and the yeast mixture. Stir with a rubber spatula until a mass of dough forms.

Dump the dough out on a lightly floured surface and knead for 8 to 10 minutes, until smooth. Do not add more than 1 tablespoon (8 g) of extra flour for dusting the surface. The more you knead, the less sticky the dough will become—it should be tacky.

Once the dough has been kneaded and it passes the windowpane test (page 117), place it in a large buttered bowl, rub the top with butter and cover with plastic wrap. Place in a warm and draft-free area and let proof for about 2 hours, or until doubled in size.

BLACKEND TOPPING: In a bowl, combine the butter, shortening, powdered sugar, flour, cocoa powder, cinnamon, vanilla and lime zest and knead until it becomes pliable. Measure out twelve balls that are 1½ tablespoons big. Place them on a dinner plate and cover with plastic wrap so they don't dry out.

ASSEMBLY: Once the sweet dough has doubled in size, press it down to release all the air. On a clean surface, measure the dough out into twelve pieces, about 95 grams each. The easiest way to do this is by cutting pieces off with a knife or bench scraper. Avoid ripping the dough or adding too many small pieces to make up one piece.

(continued)

Egg Wash
1 egg white, beaten
½ tsp water

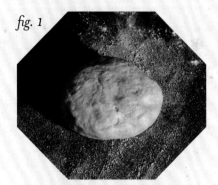

fig. 1

fig. 2

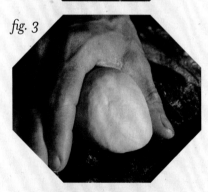

fig. 3

fig. 4

To shape each piece, gently flatten the dough into a circle (fig. 1). Gather the ends in the center and tightly pinch them together to create a pouch shape (fig. 2). Seam side down, roll the dough on the surface between your thumb and pointer finger until it is taught and forms into a ball (fig. 3).

☛ *This step is important in preventing them from busting open while they bake.*

Place them on a parchment-lined baking sheet and loosely cover with plastic wrap.

Take a ball of the blackened topping and place it in between two pieces of plastic wrap. Flatten it into a disk large enough to cover the top and most of the sides of the sweet dough balls. Gently peel the topping off and add it to the top of a dough ball. Repeat until all twelve dough balls have been covered. Inscribe a swirl pattern on top of the black topping with a paring knife (fig 4). Don't cut too deep.

☛ *To get perfect swirls, place a bun in the center of a cake turntable. Very slowly spin the turntable while inscribing the swirl with a pairing knife from the center to the end of the bun.*

EGG WASH: Prepare the egg wash by mixing the egg white and water until loosened. Gently brush the tops of the dough balls with the egg wash and lightly cover with plastic wrap. Let the bread proof for 40 to 45 minutes. The black dough should start to crack a bit. Meanwhile, preheat the oven to 350°F (180°C).

Bake the buns for 20 to 23 minutes, or until the internal temperature is 200 to 205°F (90 to 95°C) when checked with an instant-read thermometer. Transfer the Mourning Buns to a wire rack to cool.

Enjoy these with coffee or store in an airtight container for up to 2 days. Either way, they're to die for.

TOAD BREAD

TOAD-SHAPED BREAD WITH A GOLDEN CRUST CROAKS, FROM THE OVEN WITH A SMELL SO ROBUST. COVERED WITH GARLIC AND ROSEMARY TOO, THIS TOAD IS PERFECT TO MOP UP YOUR STEW.

Yield: 1 *toad loaf*

Dough

100 g (⅓ cup + 2 tbsp) whole milk

100 g (⅓ cup + 2 tbsp) water

14 g (1 tbsp) granulated sugar

9 g (2¼ tsp) active dry yeast

400 g (3½ cups + 2 tbsp) bread flour, sifted

9 g (1½ tsp) kosher salt

14 g (1 tbsp) vegetable shortening

14 g (1 tbsp) unsalted butter, softened

2 tsp (10 g) apple cider vinegar

1 large egg

4 g (1 tbsp) fresh rosemary, chopped

DOUGH: In a saucepan or in the microwave, warm the milk and water between 105 and 110°F (40 and 43°C). Stir in the sugar until it dissolves, then add the yeast. Let it sit for 5 minutes, until the mixture starts to foam at the surface. This is a sign that the yeast is alive and ready to use.

In a large mixing bowl, add the flour, salt, shortening, butter, vinegar, egg, rosemary and yeast mixture. Stir with a rubber spatula until it clumps together into a mass. Turn the dough out onto a clean surface and knead by hand for 10 minutes. Refer to the How to Knead section in Bread Basics (page 116). Place the dough in a large buttered bowl and cover with plastic wrap. Let it proof for 1½ hours in a warm and draft-free area until it doubles in size.

☛ *Proof the dough in the bowl in a microwave that is turned off to prevent drafts or sudden temperature changes.*

Once the dough has risen, gently punch it down to release all the air. Remove a nickel-sized amount of dough from the bottom. Cut it in half and roll into little balls. Set them aside for the eyes. To form the toad, roll the large portion of dough into an oval egg shape. Place it on a parchment lined baking sheet (fig. 1).

Cut notches in the dough ball on four sides and open them up (fig. 2). Cut four notches in the middle of the first notches. Open the notches up to reveal the legs (fig. 3 and 4). Flip the back legs forward so they point in the direction of the head.

Use scissors to cut notches into the legs to imitate fingers and toes (fig. 5). Crimp the exposed edges of the toad and shape the edges to define the form. Smooth out any rough geometric angles. Poke two holes into the head and use the bits of dough you pulled off from earlier to make eyes (fig. 6).

☛ *Keep in mind that the toad will expand during proofing. Make the features such as the arms and legs skinny as well as the torso.*

(continued)

TOAD BREAD *continued*

Garlic Egg Wash

1 egg yolk

1 tsp water

A pinch of salt

¼ tsp garlic powder

Rosemary Garlic Butter

113 g (½ cup/1 stick) unsalted butter, softened

4 g (1 tbsp) fresh rosemary

1 tbsp grated Parmesan cheese

¼ tsp garlic powder

¼ tsp kosher salt

GARLIC EGG WASH: Mix the egg yolk, water, salt and garlic powder. Gently brush the toad evenly with the egg wash, making sure not to deflate the dough. Cover the toad with plastic wrap that has been sprayed with nonstick cooking spray. Leave it to rise for 30 to 40 minutes, until it doubles in size.

Bake the bread at 350°F (180°C) for 28 to 30 minutes. When an instant-read thermometer poked from the backside into the center reads 200 to 205°F (90 to 95°C), it is done. Immediately transfer the toad to a cooling rack and let it cool completely before slicing, about 1½ hours.

ROSEMARY GARLIC BUTTER: Mix the butter, rosemary, Parmesan, garlic powder and salt. Wrap the mixture in plastic wrap and shape into a sausage. Refrigerate until the consistency is spreadable.

Once the bread has cooled, serve it with the rosemary garlic butter, soup or stew and enjoy. Store any leftovers in plastic wrap away from the air for 1 to 2 days.

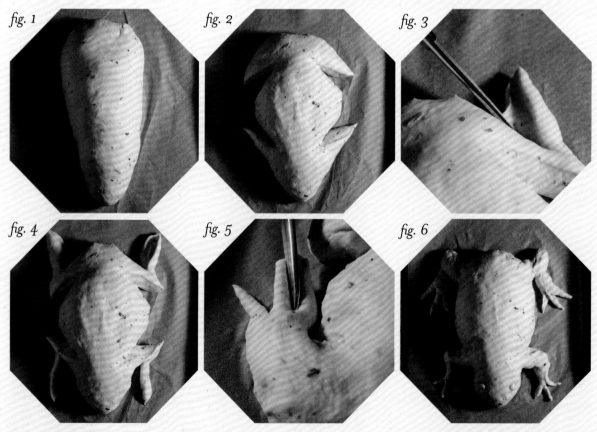

fig. 1 fig. 2 fig. 3

fig. 4 fig. 5 fig. 6

BLOODY BEIGNETS

GOLDEN AND SOFT, THIS DEEP-FRIED CONFECTION. BURIED BENEATH A SUGARY SNOW. RASPBERRY BLOOD, CRIMSON PERFECTION. BEAUTIFULLY SPLATTERED WITH ONE SINGLE BLOW.

Yield: About 20 small beignets

....

Dough

4 cups (500 g) all-purpose flour, plus more for dusting

1½ tsp (9 g) kosher salt

1¼ cups (270 g) whole milk

⅓ cup (73 g) brown sugar

2 tsp (8 g) vanilla extract

2½ tbsp (35 g) unsalted butter, melted, plus more for brushing

1 tbsp (12 g) active dry yeast

1 large egg, lightly beaten

Vegetable oil, for frying

Raspberry Bloody Sauce

12 oz (340 g) frozen raspberries

½ cup + 1 tbsp (114 g) granulated sugar

2 tsp (8 g) vanilla extract

2 tsp (10 g) lemon juice

Red and green food dye

1 tsp cornstarch

1 tsp cold water

Powdered sugar, for dusting

DOUGH: In the bowl of a stand mixer, sift together the flour and salt, then set aside. In a microwave-safe glass measuring cup, warm the milk to 105 to 110°F (40 to 43°C). Add the brown sugar, vanilla and butter and stir. Then add the yeast and mix until dissolved. Let it sit for 5 minutes to foam up. Make a well in the center of the flour and pour in the yeast mixture along with the lightly beaten egg. Attach the dough hook and knead on medium speed for 8 to 10 minutes, until the dough is soft and smooth. Add the dough to a large buttered bowl, then butter the top of the dough and cover it with plastic wrap. Let it rise in a warm and draft-free place for 1 hour, or until it doubles in size. Meanwhile, make the bloody sauce.

☞ *Proof the dough in the bowl in a microwave that is turned off to prevent drafts or sudden temperature changes.*

RASPBERRY BLOODY SAUCE: In a small saucepan, add the frozen raspberries and sugar. Cook over medium heat until the raspberries have thawed and the mixture starts to simmer. Remove the raspberries from the heat, pour them into a blender and blend until smooth. Strain the mixture back into the saucepan to remove any excess skin and seeds. Add the vanilla, lemon juice, one drop of red food dye and a very small dab of green food dye to create a blood color. Bring the mixture back up to a simmer. In a small prep bowl, mix the cornstarch and cold water to create a slurry. Pour it into the simmering raspberry puree. Mix it in vigorously until the mixture thickens. Pour it into a bowl to cool.

Once the dough has risen, punch it down to release the air bubbles. Turn it out on a lightly floured surface. Roll the dough out in a rectangle to ¼-inch (6-mm) thickness. Cover it with plastic wrap and let rest for 30 minutes.

(continued)

BLOODY BEIGNETS *continued*

During the last 15 minutes of rest, heat about 3 inches (8 cm) of vegetable oil in a cauldron to 350°F (180°C). Cut the dough into your desired square size with a pizza cutter. Fry the dough for 30 seconds to 1 minute per side, until golden brown. **Only** fry up to two squares at a time. Any more and the temperature of the oil will drop. It is important to maintain a temperature between 350 and 360°F (180 and 183°C). If the heat is too high, they will burn; if it is too low, they won't puff up.

Once they have fried, take the beignets out with tongs and lay them on a baking sheet lined with paper towels. Sift on a generous amount of powdered sugar and splatter with raspberry bloody sauce. These are best served fresh, so enjoy them while they are hot.

PUMPKIN SPICE BRIOCHE ROLLS

ESSENCE OF AUTUMN ENCASED IN A ROLL. SOFT, GOOEY TEXTURES AWAKEN THE SOUL. BAKED TO PERFECTION, A HUE SO ENTICING, IT'S GOLDEN AND SWEET AND COVERED IN ICING.

Yield: **8 jumbo rolls**

....

Water Roux (Tangzhong)

50 g (⅔ cup + 2 tbsp) bread flour, sifted

160 g (⅔ cup) whole milk

60 g (¼ cup) water

1 (15-oz [425-g]) can pumpkin puree

Pumpkin Brioche Dough

80 g (¼ cup +2 tbsp) whole milk

70 g (⅓ cup) dark brown sugar, divided

9 g (2¼ tsp) active dry yeast

540 g (4¾ cups +2 tbsp) bread flour, sifted

60 g (½ cup) all-purpose flour

12 g (2 tsp) kosher salt

1 large egg

60 g (¼ cup) full-fat sour cream

10 g (2 tsp) lemon juice

50 g (3½ tbsp) unsalted butter, softened

Measure out all the ingredients and have all equipment handy before beginning.

WATER ROUX: Add the flour, milk and water to a saucepan and whisk vigorously until the flour is dissolved. Heat the mixture on medium heat and stir constantly, until it begins to thicken and the temperature on a thermometer reads 150°F (60°C). At this point, immediately remove the pan from the heat and whisk until the mixture is thick like pudding. Pour it into a bowl and cover with plastic wrap to cool down.

☞ *Water roux (tangzhong) is an Asian baking technique in which a pre-cooked flour paste prevents yeast bread from going stale as quickly. It also assists in giving bread a soft, dreamy texture.*

PUMPKIN PUREE: Place the pumpkin puree in a pan over medium heat. Stir constantly to reduce it down to 225 grams (¾ cups). This should take 8 to 10 minutes. Dump it out on a plate and spread in a thin layer. Place it in the freezer for 10 minutes to cool down. Take note that this will be divided between the bread dough and filling.

PUMPKIN BRIOCHE DOUGH: In a saucepan or in the microwave, warm the milk between 105 and 110°F (220 and 230°C). Stir in 1 teaspoon of the brown sugar until dissolved, then mix in the yeast. Let it sit for 5 minutes, until the mixture starts to form foam on the surface. This is a sign that the yeast is alive and ready to use.

In the bowl of a stand mixer, add the bread flour, all-purpose flour, remaining brown sugar, salt, 130 grams (½ cup) of the cooled pumpkin puree, egg, sour cream, lemon juice, water roux and yeast mixture. In a stand mixer with the dough hook attachment, mix on low speed for 1 minute, until the ingredients start to incorporate. Switch to medium speed to knead the dough for 8 to 10 minutes. The dough should look silky and elastic.

(continued)

Pumpkin Spice Filling

110 g (½ cup) brown sugar

28 g (2 tbsp) butter, softened

24 g (2 tbsp) sour cream

½ tsp vanilla extract

6 g (1 tbsp) pumpkin pie spice

¼ tsp salt

63 g (½ cup) all-purpose flour, plus more for dusting

Sour Cream Glaze

120 g (1 cup) powdered sugar

3 tbsp (36 g) sour cream

28 g (2 tbsp) melted butter

¼ tsp vanilla extract

1 drop orange food dye

Special Tools

Instant-read thermometer

Dental floss or thread

fig. 1

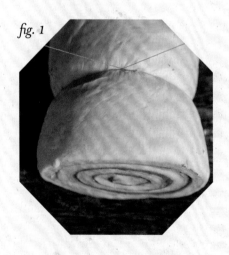

Take the bowl off the mixer stand, then squash the butter into the dough with your hands in a clawing motion. It's messy, but this helps the dough incorporate with the butter easier. Add the bowl back onto the stand mixer and knead it on medium speed for 5 more minutes.

Dump the dough out on a lightly floured surface and bring it into a smooth ball. Place it in a large buttered bowl and cover with plastic wrap. Let it proof for 1 to 1½ hours in a warm and draft-free space, until doubled in size.

PUMPKIN SPICE FILLING: In a small bowl, whisk together 65 grams (¼ cup) of the cooled pumpkin puree, brown sugar, butter, sour cream, vanilla, pumpkin pie spice, salt and flour into a paste. Cover and set aside.

SHAPING: After the dough has risen, punch it down to release all the air bubbles. Turn it out on a lightly floured surface, then pat and roll it into a 15 x 22–inch (38 x 55–cm) rectangle. Spread on the pumpkin spice filling evenly and roll it up tightly.

Use some floss or thread to cut the slices. Slide the floss under the dough, then take each end of floss in the opposite hand and cross them over each other. Pull tight in one quick motion to cut through the dough (fig. 1).

Place the slices on a parchment-lined baking sheet 2 inches (5 cm) apart. Cover with plastic wrap and let rise for 30 to 45 minutes, until they double in size. Meanwhile, preheat the oven to 350°F (180°C).

SOUR CREAM GLAZE: In a bowl, whisk together the powdered sugar, sour cream, melted butter, vanilla and orange food dye. Cover and set aside.

Once the dough has risen, bake for 25 to 30 minutes, or until an instant-read thermometer reads 190°F (88°C) when stuck in the center of the bread from the side. Immediately cover with a thin layer of the sour cream glaze.

Because the glaze contains dairy, any leftovers must be refrigerated. It's best to only glaze as many rolls that are going to be eaten that day. Unglazed rolls can be stored wrapped up tight on the counter and at room temperature for 2 to 3 days, and the remaining glaze can be stored in the refrigerator. Leftovers can be reheated for 5 seconds in the microwave then re-glazed. Enjoy the ooey gooey goodness of autumn.

FAROLITO BREAD

(BREAD IN A BAG)

MIXED IN A BLENDER AND BAKED IN A BAG, A FESTIVE BREAD COMES TO LIGHT. THEY GUIDE A PATH TO A TURQUOISE TOWN, STUDDED WITH PINE NUTS AND CINNAMON'S MIGHT.

Yield: 1 loaf

Melted butter, for brushing paper bag

Bread Batter

375 g (3 cups) all-purpose flour

¾ tsp kosher salt

100 g (½ cup) granulated sugar

½ tsp orange zest

260 g (1 cup + 3 tbsp) whole milk

9 g (2¼ tsp) active dry yeast, divided

1 large egg

1 egg yolk (save the white)

38 g (3 tbsp) vegetable oil

½ tsp vanilla extract

120 g (1 cup) toasted piñon (pine nuts), divided

fig. 1

Prepare the paper bag by placing two paper bags inside of each other. Fold the edges down about 1½ inches (4 cm) until the bag reaches 6¾ inches (17 cm) tall. This size is important; it's so the dough doesn't overflow while baking. Brush the inside of the bag with a generous amount of melted butter.

Lightly tie two pieces of bakers' twine around the bag. The first right below the top fold and the second about 2½ inches (6 cm) from the bottom. This keeps the bag from distorting as the dough rises (fig. 1). Place it on a baking sheet and set it aside.

BREAD BATTER PART 1: In a large bowl, whisk together the flour and salt and set aside. In a small bowl, add the sugar and orange zest. Pinch the orange zest into the sugar with your fingertips. This releases citrus oils into the sugar. Set it aside.

In a microwave-safe measuring cup, heat the milk to 105 to 110°F (40 to 43°C). To the warm milk, mix in 1 teaspoon of the orange sugar and the yeast. Let it sit for 5 minutes, until it becomes foamy. To a blender, add the egg, egg yolk, oil, vanilla, remaining orange sugar and yeast mixture. Mix in a blender for 2 minutes exactly. Make a well in the center of the flour and add the liquid mixture. Stir with a wooden spoon until the flour is combined and the batter has a little bit of resistance to it when mixed. This is supposed to look like a thick batter and not a ball of dough. Scrape the sides of the bowl, cover with plastic wrap and leave the batter to rise in a warm place for 45 minutes to 1 hour, until doubled in size. Meanwhile, prepare the cinnamon paste and toast the pine nuts.

(continued)

FAROLITO BREAD *continued*

Cinnamon Paste
1 egg white
42 g (3 tbsp) dark brown sugar
8 g (1 tbsp) ground cinnamon
¼ tsp kosher salt
39 g (3 tbsp) butter, melted
31 g (¼ cup) all-purpose flour

Anise Butter
1 tsp anise seeds
113 g (½ cup/1 stick) salted butter, softened
¼ tsp cinnamon
24 g (3 tbsp) powdered sugar
21 g (1 tbsp) honey

Special Tools
2 brown paper lunch bags
Bakers' twine
Pastry brush
Pie plate or casserole dish
Instant-read thermometer
Mortar and pestle

To toast the pine nuts, add them to a pan over medium heat and stir constantly until fragrant. Dump them on a plate to cool, then divide them into three portions: ¾ cup (90 g) for the batter, 2 tablespoons (15 g) for the topping and 2 tablespoons (15 g) for the anise butter.

CINNAMON PASTE: To a bowl, add the egg white from earlier, brown sugar, cinnamon, salt, melted butter and flour. Mix with a fork until smooth and set it aside for later.

BREAD BATTER PART 2: Once the batter has risen, stir it with a wooden spoon to release all the air bubbles. The batter should be a lot thicker now, so this requires some elbow grease. Add the ¾ cup (90 g) of toasted pine nuts and mix them in until dispersed. Using a cookie scoop that holds about ½ cup, add a scoop of batter to the bottom of the paper bag. If you don't have a cookie scoop, lightly butter ½-cup measuring cup and use a spoon to assist with getting the batter out of the measuring cup and into the bag. Butter your fingertips with melted butter and lightly press the batter flat into the bag until it is even.

Add a quarter of the cinnamon paste and use a pastry brush to spread it on top of the batter. It is helpful to dip the pastry brush in a bit of melted butter to make spreading the paste easier. It doesn't have to be even. Repeat this layering until all the batter is used up and you end with a layer of cinnamon paste on top. Sprinkle with the 2 tablespoons (15 g) of toasted pine nuts, cover the top with plastic wrap and place the bag on a baking tray. Let it rise in a warm, draft-free place for another 45 minutes to 1 hour.

Proof the dough in the bowl in a microwave that is turned off to prevent drafts or sudden temperature changes.

While the dough is rising, adjust the oven racks, placing one at the lowest level and the second on the level right above. Place an empty pie plate or casserole dish on the lower rack. Preheat the oven to 425°F (220°C). Boil water in a kettle. Once the bread is done rising, add the boiled water to the dish on the bottom rack in the oven. This will create steam during baking.

☞ *If your oven only has one rack, use a narrow bread pan and place it on the side of the rack.*

Carefully place the baking tray with the bread on the top wrack and bake at 425°F (220°C) for 10 minutes. Then lower the temperature to 355°F (180°C) and bake for 10 more minutes. After this, lightly tent the top of the bread with a piece of aluminum foil to keep it from browning too quickly. Bake for an additional 15 to 20 minutes, until an instant-read thermometer inserted into the middle reads 200 to 205°F (96°C). Let the bread sit for 10 minutes, then lay it on its side to cool for about 1½ hours. Meanwhile, make the anise butter.

ANISE BUTTER: Grind the anise seeds into a powder using a mortar and pestle. To a small bowl, add the butter, ground anise seeds, cinnamon, powdered sugar and honey. Stir until combined, then mix in the 2 tablespoons (15 g) of toasted pine nuts. Dump the butter onto plastic wrap and shape it into a small log by twisting the ends of the plastic wrap. If the butter is too soft, refrigerate it for 30 minutes to firm it up a bit.

Once the loaf is completely cool, peel back the paper bag and cut it on its side like a loaf of bread. Serve with anise butter and enjoy a slice of Santa Fe. Store any leftovers in an airtight container to keep it from drying out for up to 2 days. This bread makes a great gift when wrapped up in cellophane and tied with a bow.

Farolitos are simple Christmas decorations that line the adobe houses and streets of New Mexico. The little lanterns are made up of brown paper bags filled with sand and illuminated with candles. This orange and piñon—flavored bread with anise butter is an homage to all the magical Christmases I've had in my hometown of Santa Fe, NM.

Apple Rose Strudel

A SIMPLE TAKE ON A FAMOUS DISH, IT'S EASILY CONJURED BY A SIMPLE WISH. SPICED APPLES ROLLED IN THE FLAKIEST DOUGH, THIS MEDLEY OF ROSES STEALS THE SHOW. WITH TOASTED PECANS SCATTERED THROUGHOUT, THIS TREAT IS PURE MAGIC WITHOUT ANY DOUBT.

Yield: 1 (13-inch [33-cm]) log

....

Apple Filling

⅓ cup (75 g) unsalted butter, divided

1 lb (454 g) apples (a firm variety is best)

½ cup (110 g) dark brown sugar

½ tsp cinnamon

¼ tsp cardamom

¼ tsp nutmeg

¼ tsp ginger

½ tsp salt

1 tbsp (15 g) lemon juice

1 tsp vanilla

2 tbsp (20 g) cornstarch

2 tbsp (30 g) water

Pecan Filling

2 ½ cups (315 g) whole pecans

¼ cup (50 g) granulated sugar

1 (16-oz [454-g]) box phyllo dough

1 sheet puff pastry, thawed

¼ cup (56 g/½ stick) melted browned butter, for brushing

Powdered sugar, for dusting

APPLE FILLING: To brown the butter, add it to a small pan over medium heat. Gently swirl the pan so the butter melts evenly. When the butter starts to bubble, stir it with a rubber spatula to keep the mixture moving. As soon as it turns a caramel color and the aroma smells like toasted nuts, it is done. Immediately transfer it to a bowl, including the little burned bits (they hold all the flavor), and set it aside.

Peel, core and cut the apples into ¼-inch (6-mm) chunks. Place them in a medium saucepan with the brown sugar, cinnamon, cardamom, nutmeg, ginger, salt, lemon juice, vanilla and 1 tablespoon (14 g) of the brown butter. Cook for 5 to 7 minutes, until the apples are swimming in juice. Make sure not to overcook the apples. Create a slurry by mixing the cornstarch and water in a small bowl. Add it to the apples and stir until thickened. Remove from the heat and place it in a bowl to cool completely.

PECAN FILLING: Add the pecans to a pan over medium heat and stir constantly until a nutty aroma fills the air, 3 to 5 minutes. Cool and finely chop the pecans into bits with a food processor or by hand. Mix ½ cup (65 g) of the chopped pecans into the apple filling and add the remaining 2 cups (250 g) into a bowl with the sugar. Set it aside.

ASSEMBLY PART 1: Preheat the oven to 375°F (190°C) and line a baking sheet with parchment paper. Unroll the phyllo dough and lay it on a damp paper towel. Drape another damp paper towel over the top. Phyllo dough is notorious for drying out in the air very quickly. Keep it covered with a damp cloth when not in use.

(continued)

fig. 1

fig. 2

fig. 3

fig. 4

Apple Roses

1 apple, cored and quartered

Juice of ½ lemon

Raspberry jam, as needed

On a clean surface, lay two stacked sheets of phyllo dough directly on top of each other vertically. Brush with a generous amount of melted browned butter. Grab another stack of two sheets and place them next to the first two, overlapping them by ½ inch (1.3 cm) like an open book (fig. 1). Brush with the butter, then sprinkle a third of the nut mixture on top. Repeat the process two more times from the beginning. Place one last layer of phyllo dough over the last nut layer and brush with butter. Spoon the apple filling in a line along the long side closest to you, leaving a 1½-inch (4-cm) border around the bottom and the sides (fig. 2).

Fold the sides and the bottom in and roll the dough into a log (fig. 3). Be sure to be gentle because the delicate pastry can rip. It should resemble a giant burrito. If there are huge tears in the phyllo dough, brush the log with butter and fold another sheet over it to hide the crack, like food decoupage. Transfer the log to a parchment-lined baking sheet, brush with melted butter and cover with plastic wrap.

PUFF PASTRY DECORATIONS: To make the braids, cut the thawed puff pastry into thin strips about 10 inches (25 cm) long. Braid three strands at a time. Place them as desired onto the strudel log and tuck them under.

Bake the strudel at 375°F (190°C) for 30 to 35 minutes, until golden brown. Let it cool completely.

APPLE ROSES: With the slicing side of a box cheese grater or a mandolin slicer, slice the apple wedges into thin slices. The apple wedge should be cut on its flattest side for the best results. Add the apple slices to a heatproof bowl with the lemon juice and enough water to cover the apple slices. Microwave for 5 minutes, or until the apples become soft and pliable. Fish the apples out with a fork and lay them on a single layer of paper towel. Pat them dry and lay 5-7 slices in a line lengthwise overlapping each other. Brush on some raspberry jam and roll them up (fig. 4).

ASSEMBLY PART 2: Place the apple roses onto the strudel in an attractive motif. Dust with powdered sugar, cut and serve. It is best served with a scoop of vanilla ice cream or whipped cream.

For leftovers, cover with plastic wrap and store in the refrigerator for 2 to 3 days.

Black Forest Velvet Scones

Yield: 8 *scones*

....

2¼ cups (281 g) all-purpose flour

2 tbsp (20 g) cornstarch

½ cup + 2 tbsp (126 g) granulated sugar

2½ tsp baking powder

2 tbsp (10 g) Dutch-processed cocoa powder

2 tbsp (14 g) black cocoa powder

½ tsp salt

½ cup (113 g/1 stick) cold butter, cubed

1 cup (17 g) maraschino cherries, quartered

½ cup (95 g) semi-sweet chocolate chips

½ cup (120 g) full-fat sour cream

¼ cup (50 g) whole milk

1 large egg

1 tsp vanilla extract

4 drops black food dye

Make sure all the wet ingredients and butter are cold.

In a large bowl, sift together the flour, cornstarch, sugar, baking powder, both cocoa powders and salt. Add the butter and cut it into the flour with a pastry cutter until the mixture resembles coarse meal with a few pea-sized chucks of butter remaining. Toss in the maraschino cherries and chocolate chips.

In a small bowl, whisk together the sour cream, milk, egg, vanilla and black food dye. Make a well in the center of the dry ingredients and pour in the wet ingredients. With a rubber spatula, gently fold for about twenty turns until all the flour is mostly incorporated. The dough will look shaggy and have some dry spots.

Turn the dough out onto a piece of lightly floured parchment paper. Pat the dough down into a circle that is 7 inches (18 cm) in diameter and about 1 inch (2.5 cm) thick. Slide the parchment onto a baking sheet and freeze for 30 minutes.

Preheat the oven to 400°F (200°C). After 30 minutes, cut the dough disk straight across like a pie four times to get eight triangular wedges. Place the wedges on a separate baking sheet lined with parchment paper. Bake for 20 to 23 minutes, rotating them halfway through. Let them cool before enjoying. These woeful scones last up to 2 days when covered in an airtight container.

HERE LIES NAPOLEON

FLAKY PUFF PASTRY LAYERED WITH CREAM; THE PLUMP JUICY BLUEBERRIES BURST AT THE SEAMS. SHAPED AS A COFFIN, THIS MORBID CONFECTION. DEVOUR IT WHOLE! OR SECTION BY SECTION.

Yield: 6 coffins

....

Blueberry Puree

2½ cups (365 g) frozen blueberries, divided

¼ tsp ground coriander

A generous pinch of cinnamon

1 tsp cornstarch

1 tsp cold water

Pastry Cream

1 egg

1 egg yolk

A pinch of kosher salt

2 tbsp (20 g) cornstarch

¼ cup (50 g) granulated sugar, divided

¼ cup (50 g) heavy cream

½ cup (100 g) whole milk

1 tsp vanilla extract

½ tsp lemon zest

1½ tbsp (21 g) cold butter

½ cup (100 g) heavy whipping cream

2 sheets puff pastry, thawed

BLUEBERRY PUREE: Set aside ½ cup (70 g) of the frozen blueberries and lay them out on a few layers of paper towels to thaw. Add the remaining frozen blueberries to a small saucepan over medium heat. Cook the blueberries until they are no longer frozen and begin to pop. Remove them from the heat, pour them into a blender and pulverize until smooth. Strain the puree back into the saucepan with a sieve to remove any excess skin and seeds. Stir in the ground coriander and cinnamon. Cook over low heat until the mixture reduces to ¼ cup (65 g).

In a small prep bowl, mix the cornstarch and cold water to create a slurry. Pour it into the simmering blueberries and mix until thickened. Transfer the puree to a small bowl and cover with plastic wrap to cool.

PASTRY CREAM PART 1: In a medium bowl, whisk the egg, egg yolk, salt, cornstarch and 2 tablespoons (25 g) of sugar until smooth and set it aside.

In a small saucepan, add the heavy cream, milk, vanilla, lemon zest and remaining 2 tablespoons (25 g) of sugar. Cook on medium heat until the milk is warm and little bubbles form around the edge of the pan. With a ladle, slowly scoop and pour the warm milk into the egg mixture while whisking vigorously to temper the eggs. This slow addition of hot milk ensures that the eggs don't scramble. Once the milk mixture has tempered the eggs, add the mixture back into the saucepan and cook on low heat. Whisk constantly until it thickens to the consistency of pudding. Do not raise the temperature or the eggs will scramble—low and slow is the key.

(continued)

HERE LIES NAPOLEON *continued*

Royal Icing

1 cup (120 g) powdered sugar

2 tsp (10 g) lemon juice

1 tbsp (15 g) milk, plus ¼ tsp (optional)

Purple food dye

Black food dye

Special Tools

Coffin template (page 177)

Paring knife

Piping bags

Star piping tip (Wilton #18)

Toothpicks

Small offset spatula

Immediately remove the cooked custard from the heat, stir in the butter until it melts and strain it through a fine-mesh sieve onto a dinner plate. Make sure to scrape the bottom of the sieve because that's where a lot of the mixture gathers. Cover with plastic wrap, making sure to press the wrap directly on the surface of the custard to avoid skin from forming. Refrigerate for 1 hour. Meanwhile, prepare the pastry.

PUFF PASTRY: Remove the puff pastry from the box and thaw it according to the package directions. On a lightly floured surface, roll out the puff pastry to a roughly 12 x 12–inch (30 x 30–cm) square. Cut out eight coffin shapes using a paring knife and template as a guide. Transfer to a parchment-lined baking sheet and freeze them while you repeat the process with the second sheet of puff pastry. There will be "cut off" dough that can be re-rolled one time before it becomes too tough. Cut two coffins from the re-rolled dough.

Once all the coffins have been frozen for a minimum of 20 minutes, transfer them to a parchment-lined baking sheet. Place another sheet of parchment paper on top of the coffins and place another baking sheet directly on top. Baking the pastry between two baking sheets prevents it from puffing up too much.

Bake at 400°F (200°C) for 20 to 25 minutes, rotating halfway through the baking time. Transfer the coffins to a cooling rack to cool completely.

ROYAL ICING: In a medium bowl, mix the powdered sugar, lemon juice and milk until a smooth and shiny icing forms. If it's too thick, add ¼ teaspoon of milk to loosen it up. The consistency should be as thin as a classic flood-consistency icing. Remove about 2 tablespoons (18 g) of icing into a separate bowl. Color the largest portion of icing purple and the smaller portion black. This icing dries quickly when exposed to the air, so cover it with plastic wrap when not in use. Add the black icing to a piping bag.

PASTRY CREAM PART 2: Whip up the pastry cream with an electric mixer to loosen it up. Add the blueberry puree reduction and beat for 1 minute. In another bowl, add the heavy whipping cream and beat until stiff peaks form. Fold it into the blueberry pastry cream until well incorporated. Add it to a piping bag with a small star piping tip (Wilton #18).

ASSEMBLY: Group the coffin pastries into four groups of three. The top layer from each group will be coated and the others will stay as they are. Working one at a time because the icing dries quickly, spread the purple icing on a coffin piece with a small offset spatula.

Snip the tip of the black icing bag as small as possible and drizzle horizontal lines on top. Run a toothpick up and down to create a pattern before the icing begins to dry. Let it set. Repeat five more times for a total of six iced coffins.

On a plate, add a plain coffin pastry. Pipe on some blueberry cream dollops all around and in the middle. Add a few blueberries from earlier around the edges and another plain coffin on top of that. The berries will help hold the pastry up so the cream doesn't gush out. Repeat the cream process one more time and finish off with the decorated coffin layer. Once all the coffins are assembled, lightly cover them with plastic wrap and refrigerate for 1 hour so the pastry can soften a bit. The longer the better because refrigeration is crucial to getting a good texture. If eaten too soon, the puff pastry will be hard. Time in the refrigerator gives the flavors time to meld and the pastry time to soften. These are best eaten the day of, but they are still great a day or two after. Store any leftovers in an airtight container in the refrigerator.

Sinister Sweets & No-Bake Eats

"A DANCE OF INDULGENCE AND DECEPTION."

BEETLE BITES

WRAPPED IN CHOCOLATE, THESE FUDGY CRITTERS ARE DUSTED WITH HUES TO SHINE IN THE LIGHT. THEIR SINISTER LEGS MAY GIVE YOU THE JITTERS, BUT DO NOT FEAR, THEY WILL NOT BITE!

Yield: 20 beetles

....

Modeling Chocolate

1 (12-oz [350-g]) bag chocolate-flavored melting chocolate candy wafers

¼ cup (84 g) light corn syrup

Black gel food dye

Baked Chocolate Truffle

½ cup (113 g/1 stick) butter

1 cup (200 g) granulated sugar

⅓ cup (28 g) Dutch-processed cocoa powder

⅓ cup (28 g) black cocoa powder

2 eggs

1 tsp vanilla extract

¼ tsp salt

½ cup (63 g) all-purpose flour

Special Tools

Sculpting tool

Paring knife

Exacto knife (optional)

Blush makeup brush

Metallic luster dust (blue, green, purple)

fig. 1

MODELING CHOCOLATE: Though cup measurements are provided, it is highly advised that these ingredients be measured by weight. In a heatproof bowl, add the chocolate candy wafers. Microwave and stir in 30-second intervals, until the chocolate is melted, then set it aside.

Add the corn syrup to a separate small bowl and microwave for 7 seconds—do not exceed 7 seconds or the syrup will burn. Pour the corn syrup into the chocolate and gently fold with a rubber spatula until a lumpy dough begins to form. Avoid overmixing because the mixture will start to leach out grease. Transfer the chocolate onto a plastic wrap–lined plate, cover with plastic wrap and push it down into a disk. Let the mixture cool for 45 minutes to 1 hour, until it firms up. Knead on a cold surface until it is smooth and workable. Wearing gloves, dye the dough with black food dye and knead until the desired shade is reached. Cover with plastic wrap and set aside.

BAKED CHOCOLATE TRUFFLE: Preheat the oven to 400°F (200°C). Line an 8 x 8–inch (20 x 20–cm) square pan with parchment paper and spray with nonstick baking spray.

In a microwave-safe bowl, combine the butter and sugar. Microwave in 15-second intervals, until the butter is melted, making sure to stir in between intervals. Sift in the cocoa powder, then add the eggs, vanilla and salt and mix until glossy. Fold in the flour for 20 stirs, then dump it into the prepared pan.

Bake for 12 to 15 minutes, until a toothpick inserted in the center comes out mostly clean. Let cool completely before proceeding.

Crush the entire brownie into a dough. Portion the dough into tablespoon-sized balls, which will become the bodies, and ¼ teaspoon–sized balls, which will become the heads. Shape the larger ball into the beetle's body and attach the smaller ball to make the head (fig. 1).

(continued)

fig. 2   fig. 3   fig. 4

BEETLE BITES *continued*

Roll out the modeling chocolate into a thin slab and cut it into 2½ x 2½–inch (6 x 6–cm) squares. Working on a piece of parchment paper, cover the beetle with a square of modeling chocolate. Sculpt it to form around the body and cut off any excess with a paring knife (fig. 2). With a sculpting tool, add defining features like the separation of the body, the wings and little ridges on the back (fig. 3). Place the beetles on a parchment-lined tray and set them in the refrigerator to firm up.

Meanwhile, create the legs by rolling three 3-inch (8-cm) skinny logs from the modeling chocolate (fig. 4). Place the legs into a crawling formation and stick the beetle bodies on top. Add little pincers to the head and separate the tips of the legs by cutting them with an exacto knife, if desired.

Using a blush brush, brush the beetles with metallic blue, green and purple luster dusts to give them a fanciful look. Store these creepy crawlies in an airtight container for 2 to 3 days.

👉 *Modeling chocolate is shelf stable. Any leftovers can be wrapped and stored in a cool, dry place for future projects. It will harden as it sits. Re-kneading it will make it workable again.*

Edible Wishing Candles

Warmest of wishes these odd candles grant, especially when eaten after this chant. "By flame and fire, grant my desire, a sweet simple wish is what I require." Indulge in the joy of a cereal treat that's pretty to look at but better to eat.

Yield: 5 candles

Modeling Chocolate

1 (12-oz [350-g]) bag white melting chocolate candy wafers

¼ cup (84 g) light corn syrup

Gel food dye (yellow, brown)

Cereal Treats

1 cup (60 g) mini marshmallows

½ tbsp (7 g) unsalted butter

1¾ cups (60 g) rice cereal

Creamy peanut butter, as needed

MODELING CHOCOLATE: Though cup measurements are provided, it is highly advised that these ingredients be measured by weight. In a heatproof bowl, add the white chocolate candy melts. Microwave and stir in 30-second intervals, until the chocolate is melted, then set it aside.

Add the corn syrup to a separate small bowl and microwave for 7 seconds—do not exceed 7 seconds or the syrup will burn. Pour the corn syrup into the chocolate and gently fold with a rubber spatula until a lumpy dough begins to form. Avoid overmixing because the mixture will start to leach out grease. Transfer the chocolate onto a plastic wrap–lined plate, cover with plastic wrap and push it down into a disk. Let the mixture cool for 45 minutes to 1 hour, until it firms up. Meanwhile, prepare the cereal treats.

CEREAL TREATS: In a large saucepan on medium heat, melt the butter and marshmallows. Remove the pan from the heat and mix in the rice cereal until evenly coated. Dump it out on a parchment-lined baking sheet to firm up for 20 to 30 minutes.

Grab a handful of the rice cereal mixture and form it into a thin, cylindrical candlestick shape, making sure to pack it in firmly. Shape the top to have a slight slant. Stick a wooden skewer down the middle (like a corndog). With a butter knife, spread a smooth layer of creamy peanut butter around the outside of the cereal treats. Set them on a plate lined with parchment paper and freeze for 5 to 10 minutes to firm up.

(continued)

EDIBLE WISHING CANDLES *continued*

Decoration

½ cup (95 g) white melting chocolate candy wafers

Vegetable oil, as needed

Handful of whole walnuts

Special Tools

Wooden skewers

Candle holders

Piping bags

DECORATE: Knead the modeling chocolate on a cold surface until it is smooth and workable. Dye it with the tiniest bits of yellow and brown to create an aged white color. Roll out a piece of modeling chocolate large enough to cover the entire candle. Lay the candle down on the modeling chocolate and wrap it in one smooth layer. Pinch the modeling chocolate together on one side and trim any excess with a knife, then smooth out the seam. This will be the backside. If the modeling chocolate gets too soft to work with, it is because it is too warm; try refrigerating it for 5 minutes. Repeat this step for as many candles as you require. Place them on clean candlestick holders and refrigerate for 10 minutes, until they firm up.

In a small bowl, melt the white chocolate candy wafers in the microwave in 15-second intervals, until melted. Stir between each interval to prevent the chocolate from burning. Add vegetable oil 1 teaspoon at a time until the chocolate becomes a dripping consistency like candle wax. Add the chocolate to a piping bag and cut the tip small enough to get a steady, controlled stream of chocolate. Take the candles out of the refrigerator. Pipe the white chocolate from the top of the slant and down the sides to imitate melting wax.

☞ *Wax drips down candlesticks in thin streams, so the more thoughtfully the drips are placed, the more realistic it will look.*

Cut long, thin slivers from whole walnuts and add one to the top of each candle to act as a wick. Place them in the refrigerator to set for 10 minutes.

Once everything has set, they are ready for wishing. These candles can be lit for a few seconds for presentation. They go out on their own or you can have your guest blow them out to make a special wish. Set aside the charred walnut before enjoying.

BANANA SLUG PUDDING

BANANA SLUG PUDDING'S A CURIOUS TREAT. SWEET LAYERS OF COOKIES AND CUSTARD TO EAT. AMIDST CREAMY TOPPING ARE SLIMY SLUGS DWELLING. THE SCENT OF VANILLA IS TRULY COMPELLING.

Yield: 1 (8-inch [20-cm]) dish

....

Modeling Chocolate Banana Slugs

1 (12-oz [350-g]) bag white melting chocolate candy wafers

¼ cup (84 g) light corn syrup

Gel food dye (yellow, brown, green)

1 tbsp (19 g) piping gel

¼ tsp vegetable oil

Vanilla Pudding

½ cup (100 g) granulated sugar

½ tsp salt

3½ tbsp (35 g) cornstarch

2½ cups (562 g) whole milk

2 egg yolks

1 tbsp (13 g) vanilla extract

1½ cups (350 g) heavy whipping cream

Vanilla wafers, as needed

4 medium bananas, peeled and sliced

Special Tools

Piping bag

Star piping tip (Wilton #12)

Sculpting tool

Paintbrush

MODELING CHOCOLATE: Though cup measurements are provided, it is highly advised that these ingredients be measured by weight. In a heatproof bowl, add the white chocolate candy melts. Microwave and stir them in 30-second intervals, until the chocolate is melted, then set it aside.

Add the corn syrup to a separate small bowl and microwave for 7 seconds—do not exceed 7 seconds or the syrup will burn. Pour the corn syrup into the chocolate and gently fold with a rubber spatula until a lumpy dough begins to form. Avoid overmixing because the mixture will start to leach out grease. Transfer the chocolate onto a plastic wrap–lined plate, cover with plastic wrap and push it down into a disk. Let the mixture cool for 45 minutes to 1 hour, until it firms up. Meanwhile, prepare the pudding.

VANILLA PUDDING: In a medium saucepan, whisk the sugar, salt and cornstarch until combined. Then whisk in the milk, egg yolks and vanilla until incorporated. Cook the mixture over medium-low heat and whisk constantly for 8 to 10 minutes. Be sure to never stop stirring or raise the temperature, as this will cause the eggs to scramble. Low and slow is the key. Once the mixture has thickened to the consistency of pudding, run it through a sieve into a clean bowl. Remember to scrape all the excess off the bottom of the sieve. Place plastic wrap on the surface of the pudding and refrigerate for 1 hour, until it's completely cool and congealed.

In a medium bowl with an electric mixer, beat the heavy cream until stiff peaks form. Remove 1 cup (60 g) of whipped cream from the bowl and set it aside for the topping. Beat the congealed vanilla pudding until creamy. Gently fold in the remaining whipped cream with a rubber spatula until there are no more visible streaks.

(continued)

BANANA SLUG PUDDING *continued*

ASSEMBLY: In an 8-inch (20-cm) round dish, layer vanilla wafers, pudding and bananas until the top layer is pudding. With the reserved 1 cup (60 g) of whipped cream in a piping bag with a star piping tip (Wilton #12), pipe little uniform star dollops on the surface of the pudding. Cover with plastic wrap and let the pudding rest in the refrigerator overnight or until a knife inserted into the pudding has no resistance and the cookies are soft.

BANANA SLUGS: Knead the modeling chocolate on a cold surface until it is smooth and workable. Dye half with small amounts of yellow, browns and green food dyes to get a slug color. Color another golf ball–sized portion brown. Sculpt the slugs and add little brown spots with the brown modeling chocolate. Place them on the chilled pudding. Sculpting the eyes and finer details after the slug has been placed on the pudding makes it easier to manage. Once the slugs are set in their desired positions, refrigerate for 5 minutes.

Mix 1 tablespoon (19 g) of piping gel with ¼ teaspoon of vegetable oil, then add a small dab of yellow food dye that is about the size of the tip of a toothpick. Gently brush it on the slug to add a slimy sheen.

Adding vegetable oil to piping gel helps the gel stick on the modeling chocolate, otherwise it will just slide off.

Grab a spoon and enjoy this peculiar take on a beloved classic. Cover and refrigerate any leftovers for up to 2 days.

FIRECRACKER TRUFFLES

Yield: 30 *truffles*

Truffles

1 cup (170 g) good-quality semi-sweet chocolate chips

1 cup (170g) dark chocolate bar, chopped

2 tbsp (28 g) cold butter

¼ tsp cayenne pepper (optional)

3 (9.5-g) packets Pop Rocks® candy

⅔ cup (204 g) sweetened condensed milk

1 tsp vanilla extract

TRUFFLES: Add an inch (2.5 cm) of water to a pot and bring it to a simmer on low heat. Add the chocolate chips and chocolate bar to a medium heatproof bowl. Rest the bowl on top of the simmering pot of water to create a double boiler, making sure that no water touches the bottom of the bowl. Stir the chocolate constantly with a rubber spatula. Wear an oven mitt on your least dominant hand to hold the bowl still while stirring. Once the chocolate is melted, remove the bowl from the heat and stir in the cold butter and cayenne pepper (optional). Allow the chocolate to cool until it reaches 100°F (37°C).

Once the desired temperature is met, add the Pop Rocks, folding in 1 packet at a time.

☞ *It's important to be precise with the temperature because the Pop Rocks will activate if there is too much heat.*

In a glass measuring cup, mix the condensed milk and vanilla. Heat it in the microwave in 10-second intervals until the temperature reaches 90°F (32°C). Fold it into the chocolate mixture until it starts to form into a fudgy mass, but don't overmix. Dump the chocolate onto a parchment-lined plate and even it out with a rubber spatula. Cover it with plastic wrap and refrigerate for 45 minutes, until firm and pliable. The mixture will be greasy.

Once chilled, use a tablespoon to scoop out small portions and roll them out into little balls. If the chocolate is too firm, leave it out for 15 minutes, until it softens. Place the balls on a parchment-lined baking sheet and refrigerate for 20 minutes to firm up.

(continued)

Coating

1½ cups (255 g) semi-sweet
chocolate chips

4½ tsp (21 g) vegetable oil

Gold Drizzle

2 tbsp (16 g) powdered sugar, plus
more if needed

¼ tsp gold luster dust

½ tsp whole milk, plus more if
needed

Special Tools

Piping bag

COATING: In a heatproof bowl, melt the semi-sweet chocolate chips in the microwave in 30-second intervals, until smooth. Thin it out with the vegetable oil to make dipping easier. Working one truffle at a time, place it into the bowl of melted chocolate and roll it around with the help of a fork. Fish it out and tap it on the rim of the bowl to shake off any excess chocolate. This will help prevent the truffle from getting a puddle on the bottom as it dries. Slide the truffle off the fork, with the help of a toothpick, back onto the parchment-lined baking tray. Repeat the process for all the truffles. If the dipping chocolate starts to harden, microwave it in short bursts until it's smooth again.

Once all the truffles have been dipped, place them in the refrigerator for 30 minutes to harden. Any leftover dipping chocolate can be used for decorating.

GOLD DRIZZLE: In a small bowl, mix the powdered sugar, gold luster dust and milk until it is the consistency of a pipeable paste. If it's too thick, add very small drips of milk, if too thin, add a bit more powdered sugar. Add it to a piping bag.

DECORATING: Once the chocolates have hardened, use scissors to trim off any excessive puddles of chocolate that have dried on the bottom.

These can be decorated in any fashion you'd like. This is how the ones pictured are decorated.

☞ **Gold Swirl:** Using the gold drizzle, pipe a spiral on the top. Let the drizzle dry before handling.

☞ **All Gold:** This technique is done by adding ¼ teaspoon of gold luster dust to ½ cup (144 g) of nonpareil sprinkles. Simply stick a toothpick into the bottom of the truffle, roll it around in the luster dust sprinkles and be amazed as the chocolate magically picks up a gold shimmer. Drizzle with chocolate or leave plain.

☞ **Chili Dust:** Simply sprinkle the top of the truffles with cayenne pepper.

Store these truffles in an airtight container in the refrigerator for up to 5 days. Let them come to room temperature before serving.

COOKIES & CREAM CAULDRON

DISGUISED AS A CAULDRON WITH FOG POURING OUT. A MARVEL MADE UP OF COOKIES AND CREAM.
AN ARTFUL CREATION THAT'S LUSCIOUS, NO DOUBT. SPREAD ON A CRACKER, AN EDIBLE DREAM.

Yield: 1 *cauldron*

....

Cauldron Cream

45 Oreos, divided

2 tbsp (14 g) black cocoa powder

2 (8-oz [227-g]) blocks cream cheese, softened

½ cup (60 g) powdered sugar

Dippers (strawberries, graham crackers, etc.)

Special Tools

Short, wide jar

Dry ice

Water submersible lights

Piping bag

CAULDRON CREAM: Remove the cream from the Oreo cookies. Discard the cream or save it for another use. Pulverize the cookies with a food processor or smash them in a ziplock bag with a rolling pin until they become fine dust. Pour the cookie dust into a bowl, sift in the black cocoa powder and whisk until combined. Remove ⅓ cup (45 g) of the black cookie dust and set it aside for the final coating.

In a medium bowl with an electric mixer, beat the cream cheese until smooth. Add the larger portion of black cookie dust along with the powdered sugar. Beat on low speed until the dry ingredients are incorporated, then switch to medium speed for 2 minutes, until creamy.

ASSEMBLY: Pick the jar up from the inside with your hand. Spread the mixture onto the jar with an offset spatula (fig. 1).

(continued)

COOKIES & CREAM CAULDRON *continued*

Shape the mixture into a cauldron shape. Avoid spreading it on the bottom. Place the jar on a parchment-lined plate (fig. 2 and 3).

Add a small amount of the mixture to a piping bag with a large hole. Pipe around the top of the cauldron to create a brim (fig. 4).

Place the cauldron in the freezer for 20 minutes. After it has set, pick up the cauldron by holding it from the inside. Over a plate, sprinkle the remaining ⅓ cup (40 g) of black cookie dust all around the cauldron to color it black. Place it in the center of a serving platter. Surround the cauldron with various dippers such as berries and graham crackers.

Add a water-submersible light and dry ice into the jar to imitate a brewing potion effect. Enjoy as your guests ogle at this magical spectacle.

☛ *If the water needs to be changed out to activate more dry ice, simply use a medicine syringe or turkey baster to extract some water from the jar before adding new water. Water submersible lights can be found online.*

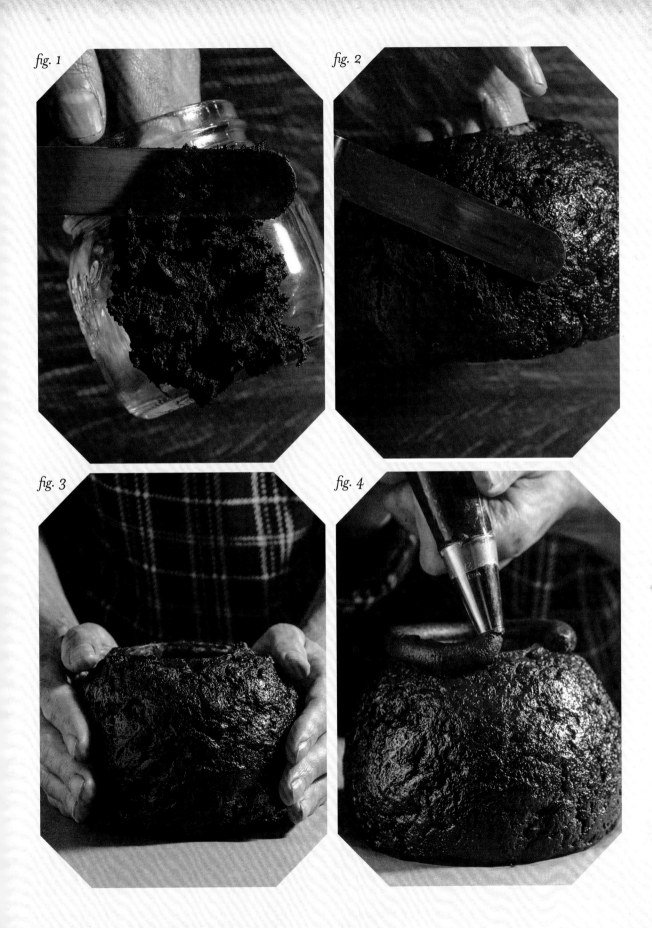

fig. 1

fig. 2

fig. 3

fig. 4

S'MORES MICE TRUFFLES

Yield: 15 mice truffles

20 whole graham crackers

1 (8-oz [227-g]) block cream cheese, softened

½ cup (60 g) jarred marshmallow fluff

1 tbsp (15 g) milk, plus more if needed

15 maraschino cherries with stems

2 (12-oz [340-g]) bags dark wafer chocolate melts

Sliced almonds

Small, round black sprinkles

fig. 1

Grind the graham crackers into dust with a food processor or by placing them in a ziplock bag and crushing them with a rolling pin. Set them aside.

In a large bowl with an electric mixer, beat the cream cheese, marshmallow fluff and milk until creamy. Dump in the graham cracker dust and mix until a soft, pliable dough forms. If the dough seems a bit dry, add a teaspoon of milk until it is the consistency of soft cookie dough.

Grab 2 tablespoons (18 g) of the mixture and flatten it into a circle with the palm of your hand. Add a cherry to the center, making sure that the stem is sticking out. Gently shape the dough into an egg shape with the cherry stem sticking out of the wider side (fig. 1). Lay the egg shape on its side to create the base of the mouse. Another option would be to make standing mice by tailoring the thinner part of the egg upward with a bend to create a neck.

Once all the mice have been shaped, melt the chocolate. Depending on the brand of wafer chocolate melts you use, the thickness varies. Most wafer chocolate can be thinned out by adding a tablespoon (14 g) of vegetable oil to the chocolate for easier dipping. Dip the pointy ends of two sliced almonds in chocolate and stick them into the head to create the ears. Place all the mice on a parchment-lined tray and freeze them for 10 minutes to harden slightly. Once chilled, coat the mice by holding them by their tails to dunk them into the melted chocolate. While holding the cherry stem, use a fork to help fish it out. Tap the fork on the edge of the bowl to remove any excess chocolate before placing it back on the parchment paper to dry. Remove as much excess chocolate as possible to get the cleanest finish and avoid puddling.

Once the truffles dry, you can add texture by scraping the surface with a toothpick or texture tool. Pipe little beads of chocolate to attach the sprinkles to create eyes and a nose. Let the mice harden before enjoying. Store in the refrigerator in an airtight container for 3 to 5 days.

POISONED PEARS

Yield: 8 poisoned pears

....

8 firm Anjou or Bosc pears (see Note)

Spicy Nut Topping
1 cup (125 g) chopped walnut pieces

½ tsp cayenne pepper (optional)

Caramel
1 cup (226 g/2 sticks) salted butter

2 cups (440 g) packed brown sugar

1 cup (340 g) light corn syrup

1 (14-oz [397-g]) can sweetened condensed milk

½ tsp vanilla extract

Icing food dye (black, purple)

Edible glitter (optional)

Special Tools
Sticks and twigs (clean)

Instant-read thermometer

Tongs

WITH FANCY PEAR AND SPICE APLENTY, THIS CARAMEL TREAT IS NOT LIKE ANY. AN IRREGULAR SHAPE AND A BLACKENED GLARE WILL CATCH YOUR EYE AND MAKE YOU STARE. BUT DEAREST READER, DO BEWARE THE SECRET OF THIS POISONED PEAR.

PREP THE BRANCHES: Gather and clean good, strong branches. Using real branches adds an extra element of wonder to these pears. Washing them with soap and water, then boiling them for 10 minutes will kill any germs. Lay them out on a kitchen towel to dry a bit.

PREP THE PEARS: Fill a medium pot with water and bring it to a boil. Add ¼ cup (60 g) of white vinegar, then add the pears one at a time to the boiling water for no longer than 10 seconds. Immediately remove the pear with tongs and place it on a cotton tea towel. Gently rub the wax off, making sure not to puncture or remove the pear's fragile skin. Remove the stem and impale the top of the pears with a clean branch. Place the pears in the freezer for 20 minutes while preparing the caramel.

SPICY NUT TOPPING: Add the walnuts to a nonstick pan on medium-low heat and stir the nuts constantly until fragrant, 2 to 4 minutes. It is easy to burn them, so keep a watchful eye on the pan. Once the nuts are toasted, dump them into a bowl and toss with the cayenne pepper, if desired. Set it aside.

CARAMEL: To a large nonstick pot, add the butter, brown sugar, corn syrup and sweetened condensed milk. Over medium-low heat, constantly stir the mixture with a rubber spatula to avoid burning. Cook the caramel until the temperature reaches 240°F (115°C). Once the caramel reaches its target temperature, remove the pot from the heat and quickly stir in the vanilla, food dye and edible glitter, if desired.

Dip the cold pears in the caramel mixture until they are fully covered. Let the excess drip off by tapping the stick on the edge of the pot. Quickly dip the bottom of the pears in the spicy walnuts. You may have to press the walnuts onto the caramel for a uniform presentation. Place the pears on a parchment-lined baking sheet and refrigerate until the caramel has set, about 15 minutes. Store them in the refrigerator for 2 to 3 days.

The type of pear matters. Firm Anjou and/or Bosc pears hold up better than Bartlett pears, which can be a bit soft. If the pears are too soft, they will slide off the stick while dipping.

CEREAL POPCORN BALLS

PRESSED INTO A LUMPY BALL, POPCORN, CEREAL AND CARAMEL COMBINED. MAKE THEM BIG, OR MAKE THEM SMALL, THIS CRUNCHY TREAT AS OLD AS TIME.

Yield: 12 small or 6 jumbo balls

Popcorn

Butter, for the bowl

3 tbsp (42 g) vegetable oil

⅓ cup (75 g) white popcorn kernels (see Note)

2 cups (75 g) cereal (no marshmallows)

Caramel

¼ cup (50 g) granulated sugar

¼ cup (60 g) brown sugar

¼ cup (60 g) water

2 tbsp (44 g) light corn syrup

1 tbsp (14 g) butter

½ tsp white vinegar

¼ tsp kosher salt

2 tsp (8 g) vanilla extract

½ tsp baking soda

POPCORN: Butter a large bowl and set it aside. In a large pot with a lid, add the vegetable oil and white popcorn kernels. Place it over medium heat, occasionally shaking it back and forth until the kernels begin to pop. Allow some steam to escape by slightly cracking the lid open from time to time. When the kernels finish popping, remove the pot from the heat. Add the popcorn and cereal to the large buttered bowl. You should have roughly 9 cups (72 g) of popped popcorn. Set it aside.

☞ For best results, use white kernel popcorn. It is more tender than yellow popcorn kernels.

CARAMEL: In a medium saucepan, combine both sugars, the water, corn syrup, butter, vinegar and salt. Stir with a rubber spatula until combined, then place it over medium heat. Cover the pot until the mixture starts to boil. Once the mixture is boiling, remove the lid and cook the mixture uninterrupted (don't stir) until it reaches 300°F (150°C). Quickly stir in the vanilla and baking soda and stir until the mixture bubbles up. Carefully pour the caramel over the popcorn and toss the popcorn with two forks (like a salad) until all the popcorn is coated. Wait 30 seconds, then begin to pack the popcorn into balls.

☞ It is recommended to do this step with latex or vinyl gloves to protect your hands against the heat and stickiness.

Place the popcorn balls on a lined cookie sheet to harden before enjoying.

Store them in an airtight container or wrap them in plastic bags with a ribbon to give them as gifts.

☞ For a traditional rendition, replace the cereal with a ½ cup of salted peanuts for a trip back to the past.

Conjuring Color

There is one thing that I know to be true about most people. They eat with their eyes first. When it comes to food art, color is just as important as the taste. It is the initial spell that tempts people to want to consume. There are a multitude of color options and techniques to choose from when coloring baked goods. Not all are interchangeable, but if used correctly, they yield such good results.

TYPES OF FOOD DYE

Gel Food Dyes

Gel food dyes are the main type of food dye that I prefer to use for food art because the colors are intense. They are readily available in most shops, and the gel consistency does not jeopardize the consistency of the final product.

Oil-Based Food Dyes

While regular food dyes either cause chocolate to seize or slide off when attempting to paint it, oil-based food dyes do the opposite. They are great for coloring and painting on chocolate because they incorporate easily without changing the consistency of the chocolate. There is an exception to this, however; modeling chocolate should be colored with regular gel food dye to avoid excess oils.

Powdered Pigments

Powdered pigments can mostly be found online in an array of colors. Also known as luster dust or pearl dust, these magical powders add metallic or pearlescent effects to your treats. They can be dusted on as is, or they can be mixed with a bit of vodka or lemon extract to create a magical, shimmer effect when used as a paint.

Natural Colorants

Natural colorants such as spinach (green), beets (pink) and black cocoa powder (black) are quite amazing. I prefer to use these in batters or glazes for a slight hint of color. Usually, natural colorants are not the most vibrant. They are dull and earthy and give off their own unique beauty.

AGING COLOR

Most times food dyes come in standard colors. I find these colors to be quite bright for most peculiar projects. You would think that the obvious choice to darken a color would be to add black or brown. This will result in the color looking dirty and muggy. A trick that I like to use to age color is using a small drop of the opposite color from my main color on the color wheel. For example, if I need to change an obnoxious sunset orange to a somber fall orange, I'd add the smallest amount of purple to deepen the color. Another example would be if I were mixing the color of blood. I would mix red with a small amount of green to get a deep red. This technique matures the color, hence why I call it "Aging Color."

EDIBLE PAINT

A drop of gel food dye with a few drops of vodka or lemon extract makes edible paint. Both vodka and lemon extract contain alcohol, which evaporates in the air and allows the color to dry. Vodka is the tasteless option whereas lemon extract will leave behind a lemon flavor. Vanilla extract may also be used for dark colors only. This paint is great to use on most desserts but is not suitable for chocolate. As mentioned before, chocolate requires an oil-based food dye to prevent the paint from sliding off.

There aren't exact measurements for edible paint. The consistency depends on the project itself. The wetter it is, the more translucent it will appear, like watercolors. The thicker it is, the more opaque it will be, like tempera paint.

INTENSIFYING BUTTERCREAM COLOR

Since buttercream is quite white, it requires a great amount of work to get the colors to be intense. Using a large amount of food dye is not desirable because it leaves a taste behind. The technique I use involves an extra step, but it makes all the difference. After preparing your buttercream, mix in a few drops of food dye (fig. 1). The color should be light. Use an immersion blender to blend the buttercream. After a few seconds, you will notice the color intensifying (fig. 2).

Let it sit for 10 minutes. The color needs some time to develop. Adjust the color, if needed, by adding a few more drops (not too much) of food dye. Blend it in with the immersion blender.

☞ *Try to avoid re-whipping the buttercream with a mixer because the color will fade once it has been aerated again.*

fig. 1

fig. 2

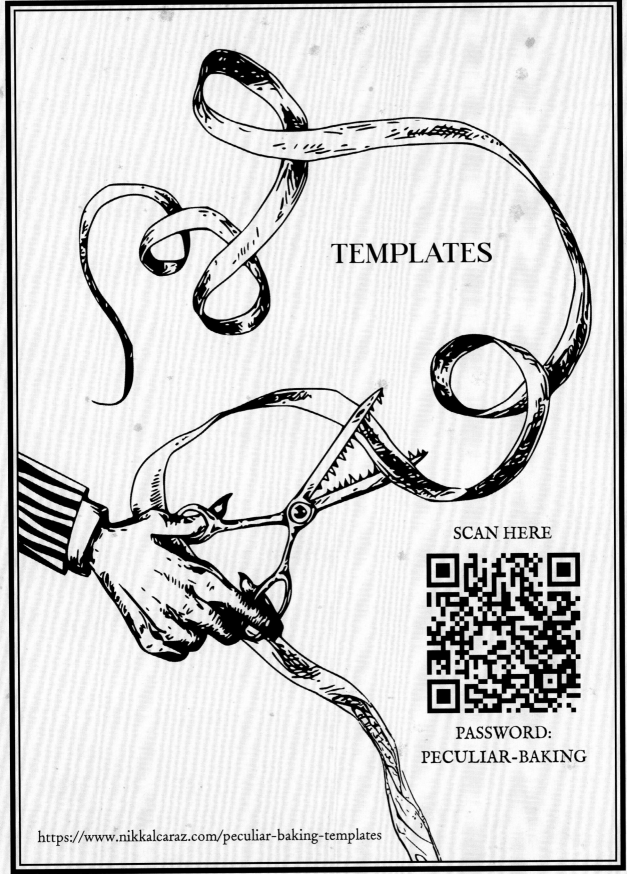

TEMPLATES

SCAN HERE

PASSWORD:
PECULIAR-BAKING

https://www.nikkalcaraz.com/peculiar-baking-templates

illustration by Mauricio Macias

ACKNOWLEDGMENTS

Quitting my day job in 2020 to follow my passion for peculiar food art was one of the scariest and most thrilling moments in my life. At the time, I had no idea where my passions would take me, but then I was met with the most wonderful community on social media. Because of your curiosity for the peculiar, this book was made possible. So here is a huge THANK YOU to the Practical Peculiarities community on TikTok, Instagram and YouTube.

To my wonderful partner Weston who encourages me every day to live my dreams without fear: Thank you for taste testing the good, the bad and the ugly desserts I've attempted throughout this whole journey. I am extremely grateful for the beautiful photos you shot for this book.

Thank you to Chef Eric at Chef Eric's Culinary Classroom in Los Angeles, for providing the extra skills and encouragement to tackle this book.

To my family, for always supporting my creative endeavors. I am truly grateful to have been raised without creative limitations.

A huge thanks to Page Street Publishing for taking a chance on me to create this book. It's an absolute dream! Special shout-out to Will, my editor Elliot and the designers Emma and Meg for helping me create this masterpiece.

I also couldn't have done it without my victi—I mean taste testers and wonderful neighbors Bruiser, Mindy and Jordan. Thank you.

Most importantly, I'd like to thank my Grandma George who has been by my side in spirit guiding the way.

ABOUT THE AUTHOR

Nikk Alcaraz, the creator of Practical Peculiarities, has been captivating audiences worldwide with his peculiar desserts and his clever mantra: "Ghosts aren't seasonal."

Raised by his grandmother in Santa Fe, New Mexico, he developed a deep appreciation for the art of baking from a young age. His fondest memories were of spending hours in the kitchen helping his grandmother bake. It was during these early years that Nikk's love for all things peculiar took root, giving birth to his distinctive style.

During the pandemic in 2020, Nikk decided to leave his 9 to 5 job to pursue his passion for food art. His imaginative approach to baking has found a home on social media platforms, where his creations have become viral sensations. He was even called a "donut" by Chef Gordon Ramsey, which he holds as a badge of honor. Nikk's ability to infuse desserts with a touch of magic and a dash of whimsy have earned him a loyal following of food enthusiasts and proud weirdos alike.

Nikk is proud to bring his debut baking book *Peculiar Baking*, where he invites you into his world of peculiar treats to instruct you how to make magic from the simplest of ingredients.

Follow him on Instagram @practicalpeculiarities and on TikTok @nikkalcaraz.

INDEX

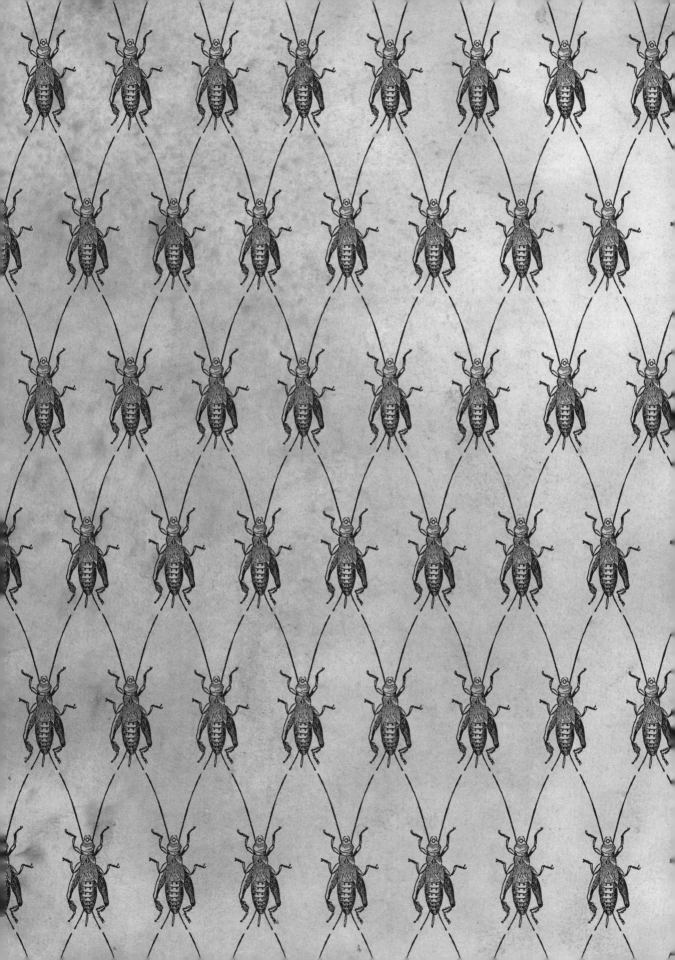